The Rugged Walker

PATRICIA KIRK, MS

Human Kinetics

ing-in-Publication Data

ISBN 0-88011-689-7
1. Fitness walking. I. Title.
RA781.65.K57   1997
613.7'176.-dc21   97-19711
                                                            CIP
ISBN: 0-88011-689-7

The "Wet Foot Test" on page 14 is adapted, by permission, from L. Micheli and M. Jenkins, 1996, *Healthy Runner's Handbook*, (Champaign, IL: Human Kinetics Publishers), 12.

The RPE scale on page 29 is reprinted, by permission, from G. Borg, 1985, *An Introduction to Borg's RPE Scale*, (Ithaca, NY: Mouvement Publications). 57.

Acquisitions Editor: Martin Barnard
Developmental Editor: Kirby Mittelmeier
Managing Editor: Jennifer Stallard
Editorial Assistant: Jennifer Hemphill
Copyeditor: Karen Bojda
Proofreader: Erin Cler
Graphic Designer: Fred Starbird
Graphic Artist: Doug Burnett
Photo Editor: Boyd LaFoon
Cover Designer: Jack Davis
Photographer (cover): Tom Roberts/Human Kinetics
Photographer (interior): Ken Probst
Mac Illustrator: Craig Ronto
Medical Illustrator: Kristin Mount
Printer: United Graphics

Human Kinetics books are available at special discounts for bulk purchase. Special editions or book excerpts can also be created to specification. For details, contact the Special Sales Manager at Human Kinetics.

Printed in the United States of America

10 9 8 7 6 5 4 3 2 1

Human Kinetics
Web site: http://www.humankinetics.com/

United States: Human Kinetics
P.O. Box 5076
Champaign, IL 61825-5076
1-800-747-4457
e-mail: humank@hkusa.com

Canada: Human Kinetics, Box 24040
Windsor, ON N8Y 4Y9
1-800-465-7301 (in Canada only)
e-mail: humank@hkcanada.com

Europe: Human Kinetics, P.O. Box IW14
Leeds LS16 6TR, United Kingdom
(44) 1132 781708
e-mail: humank@hkeurope.com

Australia: Human Kinetics
57A Price Avenue
Lower Mitcham, South Australia 5062
(08) 277 1555
e-mail: humank@hkaustralia.com

New Zealand: Human Kinetics
P.O. Box 105-231, Auckland 1
(09) 523 3462
e-mail: humank@hknewz.com

Contents

Preface

At times in my life I have felt that I had only enough energy to put one foot in front of the other. But as I venture outdoors and surround myself with nature, I become energized physically and emotionally. I have been held in love and struck in awe by the nature that surrounds me. I have learned compassion for myself on those days when I have no energy and learned to allow myself abandon, flying free down the hill, on the days I do. As I climb the rugged path up the mountain, I realize the strength I have to overcome my life's challenges. Walking the rugged path has led me on a journey that travels deep into the unfolding of who I am.

I have written *The Rugged Walker* primarily as a way of sharing my awakening—my awakening to myself and a more conscious way of living. The past five years have been a rugged walk, a journey filled with tough challenges and overwhelming beauty. Rugged walking each day up the nearby hillsides helped change my view of myself and of the world. I am learning how intimately connected I am with nature and how much it has to teach me about myself and life. As I am moved deeply by the power of the ocean, the majesty of the mountain, the wonder of the night heavens, the beauty of the rose, and the illumination of the sun, I am moved deeply by the power, majesty, wonder, beauty, and illumination that is within me, that is within each of us. Journeys must be shared so that others may be inspired to embark on their own.

Rugged walking has taught me that fitness is about living; not just about exercising or just about eating well or just about being healthy. It is about fitness of body and fitness of mind and fitness of spirit and fitness of Earth. Fitness is not about any one thing in extreme but about all things in balance. It is about having the endurance to take long walks along the beach to see the beauty of a sunset; it is about having the strength and power to climb the ocean bluff to catch a spectacular view of the horizon. It is about having the flexibility to play; it is about nourishing yourself with good food and drink; it is about having the mental alertness to debate life's issues and infuse your work with passion, whatever it is that you do. It is about treating the Earth and each other with respect, honesty, caring, and especially love; it is about having the willingness to let go of the burden of life's challenges and responsibilities and to relax, to really relax and allow self-discovery. It is about having the inner peace to let your mind soar and your creativity take spirit. Fitness is about letting go of your expectation of whom you want to become and accepting who it is you are. Fitness is about a rugged walk—journeying to see all the beauty that is around you and within you and having the energy to experience the rapture of living.

I have written this book with the hope that you may find it a fun, invigorating way to exercise and reduce stress. In this day and age, we are becoming more aware of how critical exercise and relaxation are to our health and happiness. However, many of us find it difficult to find the time and the motivation to exercise and relax on a regular basis. For a long time, many of us have felt that for exercise to be beneficial we had to exercise hard and for long periods of time. And we have never thought about the benefits of relaxation. In fact, we have believed it self-indulgent and lazy to take time to relax. But these beliefs have been proven untrue. Exercise does not have to be overly strenuous to be effective in improving our health and fitness. And any time we choose to relax is definitely important to our health as it reduces our stress, the wear and tear on our body and our mind.

The rugged walker program—providing training techniques for aerobic, muscular, and flexibility conditioning; a healthy posture; enhanced body-mind connection; and stress reduction—offers a well-rounded, motivating, and time-efficient approach to exercising. Surrounding yourself in the beauty and grace of nature is very freeing and relaxing, while playing on its obstacle course is very invigorating and challenging. One of the greatest benefits of rugged walking is that it is easy and inexpensive for everyone to do. The greatest benefit of rugged walking is that it is outdoors. Nature has a way of stimulating a new perspective on life.

So breathe. Start walking. Your rugged walking—your journey in life—is service to another, to our connected spirit. I hope we may be rugged walkers together some day.

Mary Lou O'Connor—whom I chose as my mother. Our rich relationship has provided me with the experiences through which I have come to accept and love myself. After many years together, I am your close friend and kindred spirit.

Richard Kirk—whom I chose as my father. The finest kind of man from whom I learned patience, graciousness, and a deep love for nature.

Liisa O'Maley—whom I chose as my guide through this lifetime. I am humbled by the lessons you have shared with me about the trappings of the mind, the depth and riches of the soul, and the wonder and awe of Oneness. How vast, how deep love is.

Jillian, Jane, Randy, Peter, Trudy, Gigi, Robert, Patsy, Jay, Warren—those whom I have chosen as my extended family. Without whose bright faces and open hearts, neither this book, nor my journey, would be what they are.

Warren Wertheimer—whom I have chosen as a fellow student and teacher in the classroom of life. I have grown wiser for knowing you.

Acknowledgments

I want to thank Jillian Shay, Randy Gibson, Jane Mutony, Peter Hoge, Debbie Abell, Trudy Larrieu, and Ed Larrieu who were the wonderful models for the exercises. We had a fun day and I greatly appreciate your support and your generosity of time and spirit.

Thank you Frank Meehan, a good and dear friend, for all your editing comments and most especially supportive words.

Thank you Ken Probst, a wonderful photographer.

And a particular thank-you to Kirby Mittelmeier, developmental editor, for your support, your excellent editing expertise, and most especially, for making this process a very fun and meaningful journey. Your openness and honesty were so appreciated. Your warm and happy rapport made it a joy to work with you. I never knew that publishing a book could be so enjoyable.

And thank you to Martin Barnard, acquisitions editor, for your belief in me and the project.

CHAPTER 1

A Fitness-Walking Adventure

What a gorgeous spring day! The lush, green rolling hills were beckoning. It had been a tough morning at work. Few things seemed to be going smoothly. I was beginning to feel overwhelmed. I knew exercising would help, but I had no excitement about working out in the fitness center at the club. So I decided to heed the call of the outdoors and put on my walking shoes. I have power-walked outdoors many times before, but today I wanted to experience something new, something more fun and challenging. The next thing I knew I found myself venturing off-road and up the lush, green hillside. As I climbed, I felt more and more invigorated. The terrain became more uneven, more rugged, and I was loving the physical challenge. My body felt so agile and strong. My mood picked up as I reminisced about my childhood. I climbed up and over rocks and logs, leaped over gullies, sprinted up hill, and even did push-ups against a tree and a couple of chin-ups on a branch. I felt so energized, so alive. The sky was a clear, vibrant blue. The air was fresh and light. The sun was brightly *shining and gently warm. The grass was so green. Such a sense of free-dom overwhelmed me! It was spring and everything seemed new and fresh. I felt light and happy. With each step up the mountainside, I felt the inner confidence and physical strength to overcome anything. And I realized I was ready physically, mentally, and emotionally to tackle what I had left behind at work. In fact, I was looking forward to it.*

This was the hike during which *The Rugged Walker* was con-ceived, and I felt strongly that many people would enjoy the adventure as much as I do. Rugged walking is an activity that takes you to the great outdoors to experience the fun of adventure and the conditioning benefits of exercising and to connect with the beauty and spirit of nature. It is an activity everyone can do and enjoy. Whether you are looking to ease into a more active and less stressful lifestyle or for that ultimate physical challenge, the rugged walker program can get you fit in body and mind.

The Rugged Walker is for everyone because it is easily modified for your fitness level and comfort. It is extremely convenient and affordable. With a good pair of rugged walking shoes, you can walk anywhere, anytime, and with anyone. Take your shoes with you on business and vacation trips.

Many of us want to spend our free time enjoying the outdoors with family and friends. Rugged walking is the ideal solution. Exercising with friends often makes the experience more fun and challenging. Moral support from one another is a great motivator in life and helps you stick to your exercise program. A game of "follow the leader" with friends can be a great workout, if you are willing to challenge each other to the adventure.

Full-Body Conditioning Naturally

The Rugged Walker offers a complete exercise program that provides training techniques for aerobic (cardiorespiratory), muscular, and flexibility conditioning; a healthy posture; enhanced body-mind con-nection; and effective stress reduction and meditation practice. Rugged walking provides optimal physical conditioning and may sig-nificantly help to improve your health by reducing your resting heart rate, blood pressure, stress, body fat, and physical aches and pains.

The focus of the rugged walker program is to use nature's terrain as training ground and its beauty as inspiration for variety and cross-training in order to keep exercise fun, challenging, and well-rounded. Nature offers rugged walkers the ultimate exercise studio, providing the optimal obstacle course. Hiking and low-level jogging up steep hills builds stamina and lower-body strength; climbing trees and over rocks enhances balance and agility and improves upper-body strength; leaping over mud puddles and gullies develops power and speed; stretching against a log and meditating under a tree promote flexibility of body and mind.

◈ Nature offers you the ultimate exercise studio, providing a fun and challenging obstacle course.

What makes rugged walking exciting is your own adventurous spirit. The more adventurous and creative you are with the terrain, the more challenging rugged walking is and the greater the body-mind training benefits. Rugged walking helps you remember how to play, building strength and confidence to take on life's challenges, whatever they may be.

The rugged walker program combines interval training (IT) with muscle conditioning circuits to promote endurance, power, and strength. Interval training is a very fun technique that alternates high-intensity, or more anaerobic, exercise intervals with moderate-intensity, or aerobic, intervals. The benefits of IT are improved aerobic capacity (endurance—pushing the "anaerobic threshold"), muscular fitness, and an effective workout in less time. Intense intervals include speed walking and fast-paced or power-oriented terrain drills; moderate intervals include slower-paced fitness walking and lower-intensity drills.

The 18 terrain drills presented in chapter 5—and others you can create yourself—will add lots of variety and fun to your interval training. By integrating muscle-conditioning circuits into the workout, the rugged walker program provides strength training for specific muscle groups. Resistance bands, rocks, logs, and strength-training terrain drills are used in the circuits. A series of modified tai chi exercises, which may be performed anywhere along your walk, enhance the body-mind connection while developing flexibility for enhanced fluidity and balance. Finally, a series of full-body stretching exercises enhances flexibility, while providing a great final cool-down in preparation for meditation. Meditation is an ideal way to end your workout and to reduce stress.

As a cross-training activity, rugged walking is unparalleled. Cross-training is extremely important in keeping fit. Training in different ways with different activities keeps you mentally and physically motivated and challenged. It helps you avoid burnout—of body and of mind. Rugged walking utilizes muscle groups in ways different from many other activities; therefore, you experience the cross-training benefits. Speed interval training will take your aerobic capacity to higher levels of performance. Terrain drills and exercise circuits help round out your regular muscle-conditioning program. Cross-training with rugged walking can help boost your fitness level and enhance your athletic performance in a variety of sports.

Compared with other exercise activities, rugged walking provides conditioning without overstraining the body. Structural stress and thus the risk of injury is extremely low: walking generates an impact of just 1 to 1.5 times your body weight compared with 3 to 6 times for running, for example. Walking's lower impact reduces the wear and tear of gravity, minimizing the shock impact to the body. In addition, with proper form and technique, walking promotes a healthy posture. It may seem curious to realize that there is more to walking than just simply walking, but there is. Proper form and technique make the difference. Body alignment skills and stride technique are the basics that affect one's ability to achieve the speed and power that are needed to make the workout more intense, effective, and challenging.

Rugged walking can also help bust through that weight-loss plateau by providing the body a new and stimulating activity. Fat loss occurs most efficiently when we are exercising at a moderate, aerobic level of intensity and continue to exercise for longer than 20 minutes or so at a time. Because rugged walking is very aerobic and can be done for long periods of time without the risk of injury, it is an optimal weight management activity. And as you become more conditioned, you will be able to push up your intensity, thus burning more calories in the same amount of time. (Even though higher-intensity exercise is less efficient at burning fat calories, because you are burning more total calories, you will be able to burn more fat.)

Muscle conditioning is also very important to weight loss. Muscle mass constitutes the energy-consuming tissue of your body and significantly influences your metabolic rate. Rugged walking promotes excellent muscle conditioning for both the upper- and lower-body and thus significantly stimulates metabolism. So the important thing for weight loss is to get out there and exercise.

Experiencing the Body-Mind Connection

Rugged walking takes you to some of the most inspiring places, enhancing the conditioning of the body-mind connection, which is just as important as physical conditioning. There is a very intimate relationship between our body and our mind. What affects one affects the other. Often we get distracted by our thoughts and our emotional stress about other things, that we lose our concentration on what we are doing and feeling, and miss seeing what is around us. Emotional stress robs us of our current experience: our positive outlook and our vital physical energy.

Because emotional stress seems to affect us mentally and then physically, rugged walking has proven a very effective antidote. Its rhythmic nature causes deep breathing, which is calming and brings you into focus with yourself. What better way to exercise than to play outside? Not only do getting rugged and dirty and walking and playing in nature condition your body in ways unparalleled by any other exercise equipment, but nature's energy also taps into your own inner, adventurous spirit.

◆ Exercising in nature helps stimulate a new perspective about yourself and about life.

When was the last time you leaped over a four-foot-wide ravine or a puddle in the street, jumped from a high boulder or a park bench, hiked through the forest or up a long flight of stairs, or climbed around the bluffs on the beach or the trees and planters in a park? You feel confident, carefree, and alive! Exercising outdoors helps you let go more easily of the stress in your life as the beauty of nature awakens your free and compassionate spirit. Choosing a lovely spot under a tree, along the bank of a stream, on a bluff of the ocean, or simply outside on a park bench, and meditating is an excellent way to reduce stress. Listening to the whistle of the birds, the whisper of the wind, the trickle of the water, and feeling the warmth of the sun or cool of the air induces calm energy, awakens the spirit within. As you breath in nature, whether you are far away deep in a forest or right outside your door in the city, you are in the moment, in tune with your body. You feel your body's sensations and energy. Your heart and mind slow down. As the mind releases tension and relaxes, it reciprocates and influences the body to relax. You feel your body and soul come alive with renewed energy. You feel one with nature.

Exercising in nature also reminds you of the intimate relationship between you and the Earth. When you commune with nature you often find yourself contemplating the quality of your life and the blessings of the Earth. Hiking and exercising alone in nature provide time for inner reflection. Experiencing the nature around you is an ideal opportunity for contemplating your connection with all things. Your mood is significantly affected by what you see and smell. You appreciate the beauty and harmony around you—and therefore within you. You gain a greater respect for yourself and for Mother Nature. You heighten your presence of mind, your awareness of yourself and of the moment. This awareness is critical to improving the quality of your life. Nature heightens your self-awareness because it reflects your own inner nature, your own inner physical and spiritual seasons and cycles.

I find the Earth's seasons reflect my own. In spring, I feel renewed, having been reborn out of the quiet, reflective time of the winter. Through the summer, I feel the growth and ripening of all that gave birth in the spring. I watch with gratitude in the fall as things die away and give their nourishment to replenish the Earth and my spirit. And I become quiet once again in winter to reflect on my life's journey and my heart's desire as I again wait for spring's birth.

Rugged Walking

is fun, easy, effective, and safe.
is great aerobic exercise.
promotes muscular conditioning of the whole body.
is a low-impact activity with very low risk of injury.
promotes good posture.
enhances muscular balance.
is great exercise for all ages and fitness levels.
helps the body lose weight.
promotes physical and mental health.
reduces blood pressure and lowers cholesterol.
strengthens bones.
helps reduce stress.
helps improve breathing capacity.
helps strengthen the immune system.
is the ideal cross-training activity.
is a challenging sport.
is easily mastered by anyone.
is affordable.
is convenient and can be performed anywhere.
is easily integrated into any lifestyle.
can be a great social event.
is very effective for pregnant women and seniors.
is excellent for injury and cardiac rehabilitation.
saves the environment.
enhances range of motion and reduces stiffness.
develops power and speed.
trims your figure.
allows you to take business meetings "on the road."
is mentally stimulating and helps avoid burnout.
is popular and in fitness fashion.
is a good opportunity to get to know yourself.
is an inexpensive way to sightsee.
is entertaining.
is communing with nature.
builds self-confidence and self-esteem.

is energizing.
improves circulation.
keeps you young.
helps you live in the present moment.
is a wonderful way of life.
takes you on some of the most inspiring journeys.

The Rugged Walker Challenge

Rugged walking challenges your body, stimulates your mind, frees your spirit—it is the perfect analogy to life. The best way to get anywhere in life is to take it one step at a time, to fully experience one moment deliberately and without haste. Rushing, running through life, causes you to experience only the momentum, the accelerated passing of moments, of living. You miss the rapture of life, that which is found only in the experience of the present moment. It is important to your soul to venture off-road occasionally, into the unknown, to experience the sense of mystery. It is important to challenge yourself, to climb the steep hills, to traverse life's rough terrain.

The Rugged Walker offers a program of ideas, concepts, and techniques you can use to create your own fun, well-rounded exercise adventure. I assure you, you will exercise more regularly and effectively if you find ways to make exercise convenient, motivating, easy, and fun. Rugged walking is right outside your back door. Your challenge, if you choose to accept it, is merely to take the first rugged step.

Chapter 2 shares with you how easy it is to get started rugged walking: if you can walk you can rugged-walk. Chapter 3 teaches you about proper posture, which promotes a healthy back and plays a very critical role in the effectiveness and safety of your exercise experience. Chapters 4 and 5 present flexibility and strengthening exercises, respectively, which enhance ease of mobility and balance, as well as power and muscular endurance.

The goal in *The Rugged Walker* is to turn the outdoors into your exercise studio and to use the terrain and natural environment to help you execute these exercises. Keep in mind that the exercises done on equipment created for inside a fitness center or your home merely mimic our everyday activities, and therefore they can be done outdoors. The terrain exercises in chapter 5 should help you get started. In chapter 6 you will learn how to put it all together into rugged walking programs for all levels of fitness.

The Rugged Walker also focuses on the critical importance of the body-mind connection. Exercises such as tai chi, which are presented in chapter 4, are good techniques to enhance your body-mind connection: to keep your awareness in the moment and to keep you concentrating on how you are exercising and what you are experiencing in nature. These techniques use the breath as a focal point to bring your awareness into your body. The breath is the link between your body and your mind, and by focusing on it you learn more about how your body moves and feels. The breath is also the focal point in meditation, which is an optimal body-mind technique for releasing stress and stimulating relaxation.

Chapter 7 offers guidelines for getting started and maintaining an active lifestyle and for helping you stay on course with a regular exercise program. Finally, it is very important that you take care of yourself after your rugged walks. Chapter 8 discusses the impacts of stress, both physical and emotional, in your life and provides stress-reduction and meditation techniques to help you feel more relaxed and peaceful.

Life is a rugged walk, and it is the ruggedness that is its richness. You need to pay attention to yourself and take time to condition to be able to endure the challenge and therefore to experience the joy of being healthy and fit. The benefits of rugged walking are many, significant, and immediate. Get fit now—rugged-walk. Lose weight now—rugged-walk. Reduce stress now—rugged-walk. Have fun now—rugged-walk. Rugged walking is fun and makes you feel great. And when you feel great, you are great.

2

Preparing to Rugged-Walk

To get the most out of your rugged walk, it is important to be prepared. Being prepared will ensure that your workout session is enjoyable, effective, and safe. Good rugged-walking shoes and a water bottle are basic essentials and the most important equipment for all types of walks. How intensely you plan to exercise and where you plan to go will affect what other walking gear you want to wear and bring. For example, if you plan to go for a very long, hard rugged walk, you will need a backpack with water and some light snacks, perhaps even an extra pair of socks and a T-shirt. Depending on where you plan to rugged-walk, you may want to bring your camera and possibly even your journal.

Besides being properly equipped, it is also important to be physically and mentally prepared and therefore to give some thought to the specifics of your overall exercise program and of each workout. The components that make up a well-rounded exercise program are aerobic activity, strength and flexibility conditioning, and body-mind connection techniques. In this chapter, we'll explore the roles these components play and look at how to find the right exercise prescription for you. But first, let's look at your equipment needs.

Shoes for Rugged Walkers

As you already may have experienced, having the best equipment for your sport really keeps you motivated about doing it. A good pair of rugged-walking shoes is the most important piece of equipment to your workout, so it is worthwhile investing some time and money in finding a good pair. Shoes play a major role in proper body alignment, performance, and injury prevention. They need to be specifically designed for walking and appropriate to the type of walk—rugged, speed, fitness, hike, race, and so on—you intend to perform. Rugged walking requires a lightweight, sturdy, but flexible shoe with good traction and support to manage the unstable terrain and provide you comfort and ease in performing certain drills in the workout. Rugged-walking shoes are specifically designed to absorb shock and to complement the body mechanics of rugged walking. A few tips to help you find a pair of rugged-walking shoes just right for you are listed a little later. Keep in mind that every person is different, and so are different brands of shoes. What is comfortable for one person may not be comfortable for you. The most expensive shoes may not necessarily be the best for you. Shop around.

Finding the Right Fit

There are different types of walking styles and each technique will require a specific type of shoe. Fitness-walking shoes are ideal for road or mall walking, while more rugged walking shoes and hiking boots are best for off-road terrain. Support structures, cushioning materials, and motion devices such as heel cushions, rocker soles, and medial or lateral supports are different for different shoes. For example, an off-road or rugged-walking shoe will need more traction and ankle support than a fitness or speed-walking shoe. For the rugged walker program, look for a rugged-walking shoe or lightweight hiking boot. Here are some details to look for in a shoe:

- Flexible uppers of high-quality, breathable material
- Comfortable, padded heel collar and counter
- Firm heel counter to provide ankle stability
- Well-cushioned heel for shock absorption
- Arch support
- Cushion pad at the ball of the foot for push-off
- Toe box with ample room
- Rugged or deep-tread outer sole
- Lateral support system for stability

◆ A good pair of rugged-walking shoes is important for the safety and effectiveness of your workout.

Finding the right shoe for you is easier than you think. Spend a little time assessing your own structural needs and looking for a good shoe, because good shoes are a significant factor in your adherence to your exercise program. Here are a few considerations to help assess your personal needs.

1. Do you have high or low arches? The type of arch you have will dictate the type of support you need. Support to your arches provides support to your whole body. To find out what type of arch you have, wet the sole of your foot and step on a paper towel. The imprint will show the whole sole of your foot if you have low arches or "flat feet." If you have high arches, the imprint will be of your toes, heel, and the thin outside edge of your foot. If more than a thin line of the outside edge appears in the imprint, then your arches are average.

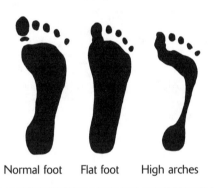

Normal foot   Flat foot   High arches

�◆ Wet Foot Test.   Adapted from Micheli and Jenkins 1996.

2. Understanding how you walk through your foot helps determine your *motion control* needs. While walking, people's feet either supinate (fall outward at the ankle), pronate (roll in at the ankle) or stay neutral (upright at the ankle). The way your feet strike the ground in walking directly affects your body alignment and posture. Your foot placement is the foundation from which the rest of your body falls in line. To avoid problems such as sore knees, ankles, hips, and back, it is important to correct for any deviation from neutral because it may cause stress to other areas of the body.

If you pronate, your foot hits the ground at the outside of the heel, and as your weight transfers through your foot, your ankle falls inward so that you push off with your big toe. A way to tell whether you pronate is to look at the sole of your shoes. Pronation wears down the outside edge of the heel and the inside of the big toe area. Supination is the opposite motion and is less common. If you supinate, you strike the ground on the inside edge of the heel then shift your weight to the outside edge of your foot and roll off your little toe. Neutral motion involves a slight pronation motion, but otherwise very little inward or outward movement of the ankle.

Both pronation and supination are inefficient ways of walking. It is therefore a good idea to wear shoes that help correct these conditions. If you pronate, look for a shoe that offers substantial arch support and a solid heel counter. You may need a *medially posted* shoe: one with a firmer midsole under the inner side of your heel. If you supinate and have a very high arch ("rigid feet"), look for more padding and softer sole material. It is a good idea in both these situations to check with a doctor to make certain that you are getting the best support.

3. When buying your shoes, identify the type of style you need and then narrow your choices to brands within your price range. Most important, consider fit and comfort. Try on the shoes for 10 minutes or so while walking around the store. This will allow your feet to adjust to the shoes and give you the opportunity to see how comfortable they really are. Some outdoor outfitters even have ramps you can stand on to test how the shoes feel on an incline: check to see that there is ample toe room.

Be certain to take advantage of knowledgeable salespeople who can be very helpful in recommending the best shoe for you. Buying rugged-walking shoes is not like buying a pair of fashion shoes. You are looking for more than a shoe that is merely your size; you are looking for a shoe that really fits. You will be putting your feet through all kinds of movements when rugged-walking, so make certain that the shoe can accommodate your personal needs. Walking-shoe salespeople are very informed about all kinds of situations regarding safe walking. They often work with prescriptions from doctors to help their clients find the best type of shoe for their needs. Ask these salespeople a lot of questions and you will certainly get an education and a good recommendation for your shoes.

4. Always make sure your shoes are in good condition. Different people wear shoes out differently. It is often advised that you check your shoes at least every six months. They will need to be replaced more often if you are an avid rugged walker. A worn-out shoe can predispose you to injury, chronic discomfort, and poor performance. If you are feeling some physical discomfort from your walking program, first check the condition of your shoes. They may not be providing the support your feet and you need.

Additional Walking Gear

Other important walking gear includes socks, relaxed-fitting athletic clothes, sunshade or sunblock, sunglasses, hat, earmuffs, gloves, snacks, camera, journal, fanny pack, and so on. Be prepared. Think about what you will need before you need it. What is the weather like? Do you need a hat against the sun or perhaps a waterproof jacket for the rain? There is a lot of neat stuff out there to make your walk very comfortable and fun. Check out walking-shoe stores like The Walking Company. You will see things such as "thermo-ties" to keep you cool on hot days, clip-on safety lights so you are seen at night, compasses so you do not lose your way, walking sticks for when you need a little support, all kinds of packs and pouches to carry your stuff, pedometers and pulse meters to monitor your pace, and great-looking hats that will keep the rain off and make you feel like Indiana Jones.

Socks can have a significant impact on comfort and preventing soreness. Once your feet start hurting, it is obviously very difficult to enjoy your workout. Today there are some very high-tech socks available. Socks are not just socks the way they used to be. Synthetic fabrics such as Coolmax, polyurethane, and acrylics are excellent for stretch, durability, and wicking away wetness. Wool, a traditional favorite, is great for keeping your feet warm and dry. Brands such as Thorlo offer these fabrics in styles that provide a fabric cushion at your heel, at the ball of your foot, and around your toes. They even have a construction that is supportive to your arch. Contrary to popular belief, cotton is not recommended for good athletic socks as it maintains wetness and causes blisters.

Take time to think about the clothes you wear. Your clothes should allow good temperature and sweat control as well as ease of movement. Again, synthetic or wool fabrics are the fabrics of choice for comfort, flexibility, and especially keeping you dry. Layering your clothes is always a good idea. If you are too hot while walking, you may fatigue more quickly. If too cold, you may feel stiff and lethargic. By layering, you have more control over your body temperature, for example, by taking off a sweatshirt when you are too hot and putting it back on when you cool down. For rugged walking you should wear roomy, relaxed, lightweight, or spandex clothing. For example, long pants may not be flexible or roomy enough for some of the rugged-walking drills. Athletic or spandex shorts may be better. Heavy jackets are also inhibiting.

Accessories such as a hat, a scarf, sunblock, sunglasses, and so on can really help make your walk safer and more enjoyable. If you are planning a long walk, be sure to take along some light snacks to replenish your energy along the way. Fruit and multigrain snacks are easy to carry and are excellent for restoring energy and satisfying hunger. Nutritional bars such as Power Bar are also great for this purpose. Water is, of course, essential on all walks (see sidebar). It is a good idea to have a belted type of water bottle so you do not have to actually carry the bottle, which can inhibit you from doing a drill or climbing over something.

Remember too that rugged walking is not merely a workout for the body, but also for the mind and spirit. Plan some walks in very beautiful places to awaken your inner energies. A small pair of binoculars gives a wonderful opportunity to observe birds or other wildlife. Take along a camera to capture inspirational sights. Taking a picture is a very meditative practice, as it causes you to stop and notice—to be aware in the present moment. Bringing along a journal is a great way to capture those inspirational moments in writing.

 ## A Word About Water

Hydration is a very important aspect of a safe, effective, comfortable walk. Adequate hydration is critical for proper metabolism and energy production, heat dissipation, and good performance. When you are dehydrated, you become

Continued on next page

A Word About Water—continued

fatigued and more susceptible to injury. You will most likely shorten your workout. Thirst is not an adequate indicator of dehydration. By the time you feel thirsty, you may already be dehydrated. Drinking water must be a conscious act rather than an instinctive reaction. The avid exerciser may be wise to drink as much as four quarts of water on exercise days, even more for longer-duration exercise in dry heat. Take along a belted water bottle. Prepare for your workout by drinking eight ounces of water approximately 20 minutes before you exercise. Stay well hydrated throughout your walk by drinking four ounces every 15 minutes, and replenish your stores with eight ounces within 30 minutes after your workout.

H_2O facts:

We all need water.

We are about 70 percent water.

Our body contains 40 or more quarts of water.

Water is essential to every biological process.

Water maintains blood volume and kidney function.

Our brain is about three-quarters water.

Water regulates body temperature.

Water is needed for healthy skin.

A loss of 2 to 5 percent of body water can seriously affect you, inducing fatigue, dizziness, headaches, and slurred speech.

A loss of 15 to 20 percent of body water may even cause death.

Dehydration can make you feel tired, weak, and unable to focus.

We lose 2 1/2 to 3 quarts of water a day from normal elimination, perspiration, and respiration.

We lose another quart for exercise 45 minutes to an hour long, much more in a hot and humid climate.

Air travel, coffee, and alcohol increase dehydration.

Components of Your Exercise Program

The body is made up of a variety of systems, each with its own particular function. It is important to condition each system so that you obtain optimal overall fitness. Specific methods of exercise are required to condition each of these systems. Aerobic training, such as walking, running, hiking, cycling, dancing, swimming, cross-country skiing, or stair climbing, is most effective in training the heart and lungs to endure. Strength training, such as manual resistance exercises and lifting weights, improves body alignment and enhances muscular strength for performance. Flexibility conditioning, such as stretches and rhythmic exercises, increases your range of motion for greater mobility, which is very important for ease of movement, good posture, and injury prevention. All of these training types—aerobics, strength, and flexibility—complete what I like to call the physical fitness triangle. If one of them is neglected the whole structure is weak and unstable. It is therefore important to integrate all of these components of fitness into your exercise program to make it complete, well-rounded, and strong. Another important component of fitness, which is becoming more widely acknowledged and more actively integrated into fitness programs, is currently referred to as the body-mind connection. This concept involves our degree of attention and concentration on our body and its sensations, for example, focusing on how your body feels while you are exercising. Body-mind concepts are discussed in more detail later in this chapter.

When designing your own exercise program, be sure to have fun and add variety. Variety is the spice of life. Cross-training is the key to variety. If you are feeling bored emotionally, most likely so is your body. Training through a variety of activities can help stimulate different muscle groups, break through the weight-loss and conditioning plateaus, and keep you motivated. It is important to vary not only the exercises, but also the intensities of your workouts. Some days you may want to stroll and meditate, while on other days you may want to tackle the terrain as a rugged walker. Exercising outdoors is a great motivator. Rugged walking is a wonderful way to get some fresh air and have fun exercising in a natural environment. The more fun you have playing in the environment, the more fun exercising will be.

The components of your exercise program we discuss in detail in this chapter are your aerobic exercise prescription and body-mind concepts. The flexibility and strength-training components of your program are discussed in detail in chapters 4 and 5, respectively.

Your Aerobic Exercise Prescription

People often seek the guidance of fitness professionals when creating an exercise program. Fitness professionals provide recommendations in the form of an *exercise prescription*. Your exercise prescription takes into account your degree of fitness, your medical status, and your personal goals and prescribes or recommends certain exercises to enhance your physical conditioning. Your exercise prescription takes into account the frequency, intensity, duration, and rate of progression of your exercise regime. Frequency is how often or rather the regularity with which you exercise, for example, three times per week. Intensity refers to how easy or how hard your exercise is, and duration is the length of time you exercise at any one time. Rate of progression measures the rate by which you advance each component of your exercise program in order to become more conditioned. The degree of conditioning you experience over time is directly affected by the frequency, intensity, and duration of your exercise. Generally, the more often and longer you exercise at a sufficient level of intensity, the more quickly you will experience conditioning or training effects as your body changes and adapts. Frequency may be the most important of these factors. If you exercise intermittently, your body will not have the chance to condition, and you will always feel as if you are starting over.

The component of your exercise program we discuss in detail here concerns your exercise prescription for *aerobic capacity*, which is your ability to endure aerobic exercise for a certain length of time and at a certain level of intensity. Your ability to endure is a function of how your heart rate, blood pressure, and oxygen consumption respond to a certain stress load or level of exercise. An aerobic exercise stress test is the best way to measure this physiological response. A stress test involves walking or running (most often on a treadmill) or biking while your heart rate, blood pressure, and oxygen consumption are recorded. The results are a measure of your level of aerobic fitness. Based on the results, your exercise prescription will recommend the safest frequency, intensity, duration, and rate of progression for your workout. Both maximal and submaximal stress tests provide excellent data from which to derive your exercise prescription. A maximal test should always be performed in the presence of a physician; it is highly recommended if you are over 40 that you have a maximal stress test prior to beginning an exercise program.

According to the American College of Sports Medicine (ACSM) guidelines, the exercise prescription for optimal aerobic or cardiorespiratory fitness is to exercise at least three times a week for approximately 20 to 60 minutes per session at an intensity of 60 to 90 percent of maximal heart rate (MHR). MHR is a measure of physiological intensity and represents the highest number of beats per minute of your heart. It is not healthy or safe to exercise at this level of intensity. Therefore, aerobic prescriptions recommend an ideal percentage, your target heart rate (THR), usually 60 to 90 percent of MHR. Exercising at your THR is necessary to cause physical adaptation or aerobic conditioning. Although the ACSM recommendation is an excellent prescription, it may be too much for beginners and therefore may not be a good place to start. ACSM has recently modified its prescription to indicate that it is best to begin an exercise program at very low to moderate levels of activity and progress gradually to more intense exercise.

You may have seen the recent publicity about the new report from the U.S. Surgeon General that states that "lack of physical activity is detrimental to your health," detrimental even to the point that some health professionals compare the negative effects of inactivity to smoking a pack of cigarettes a day. Therefore, the Surgeon General and other health and fitness professionals strongly recommend that you become more active. Research has shown that *all* activity, no matter how insignificant it may appear, is beneficial for good health, fitness, weight loss, and stress reduction. Current research tells us that many benefits may be gained from taking even a 5- to 10-minute walk at a moderate pace a couple times a day. Each time you take a walk you are releasing stress, which is a great boon to your health and youthfulness. You certainly burn more calories and work more muscles than if you were just sitting. You can be easily more active by getting off the bus before your stop and walking the rest of the way to work. Ride your bike to the store, or take the stairs instead of the elevator. As you integrate more activity into your lifestyle, you will become accustomed to it and will do more of it. The ways you choose to exercise will gradually and easily become more advanced; for example, you may walk longer and more often, do muscular conditioning exercises in the living room, join a club to take advantage of a variety of facilities and activities, take up a sport, go on more physically active vacations, buy exercise equipment for your home, and so on. Soon you will be exercising at the ACSM's recommended exercise prescription for optimal fitness, health, and weight loss. Simply becoming more active is the first and most important step to a fitter lifestyle and a fitter you.

One of the greatest factors leading to poor exercise adherence is choosing to start with a program that is too difficult and intense. By starting out too aggressively you may injure yourself or lose interest and drop out of your exercise program. The keys to ensuring that your program is safe and effective are moderation and gradual progression. If you start out too intensely, you may actually be doing more harm than good. You may be tearing down the body, making yourself susceptible to injury and illness. You may feel so sore after the first few workouts that you are discouraged from working out again. However, this is not to say that feeling a bit sore after your first workout or two means that you worked out too hard or that your workout was harmful and not effective. When first beginning your program, especially after your first weight-training session, you will most likely experience soreness. This is normal and should be expected. When the body works a bit harder than it is used to, there will be a buildup of a by-product of energy expenditure, called lactic acid, within the muscle fibers, as well as microscopic tears in the fiber, which cause soreness. It is the degree of soreness that is important. Moderate soreness is a good thing because it indicates that you have worked the body. However, if you have overdone it, you may be sore for days. You may feel more sore the second day after a tough workout, so do not be discouraged. Stretching and low-intensity activity, such as walking and riding a bike, will help relieve the soreness. And you should ease up on your next workout.

Adding Weights

You may have thought about incorporating weights into your walking program in order to increase intensity. There is no strong evidence that simply carrying weights increases intensity significantly. However, by moving the weights through a large range of motion, you can increase intensity and therefore greater caloric expenditure.

Before using weights, however, be sure to evaluate whether or not the potential benefit of using weights—increased intensity—outweighs the potential cost—possible injury. For handheld weights to be effective in significantly increasing intensity, they need to be pumped through a very large range of motion at the shoulder joint. Although this will increase caloric expenditure, this may also increase the possibility of injury to the shoulder, especially to the rotator cuff. Holding weights, particularly holding them tightly, may also elevate blood pressure and is therefore contraindicated for hypertensive and cardiac patients. Weights worn around the torso may increase intensity but need to be rather heavy to do so. They may distort proper body alignment, increasing the potential for injury. Ankle weights are not recommended because they may compromise body alignment and thus may significantly increase the risk of hurting the lower back and causing possible knee damage. It has been proven that the average healthy individual can achieve his or her THR through a vigorous walking program without the use of weights. With proper form and technique THR is usually reached within the first mile or 10 minutes of the workout. Working with speed, manual resistance, and terrain in your walking technique should provide you with optimal intensity and without the risk of injury.

Handheld weights used in specific exercises during the workout, however, can be effective for upper-body muscle conditioning. Upper-body exercises are used extensively in the rugged walker program and are a great way to add variety

Continued on next page

Adding Weights—continued

to your program. It is advised that a person have appropriate upper-body strength before adding weights to the walking program. Pay close attention to proper form and body mechanics while using the weights to avoid structural stress and possible injury.

Each exercise session needs to have its own rate of progression, beginning slowly with a warm-up, gradually increasing in intensity, and then slowing down for cool-down, final stretch, and meditation. The warm-up should include low-intensity aerobic activity, such as walking, combined with rhythmic, large-range-of-motion exercises for the whole body (such as slow, large arm circles, overhead reaches, and lunges). The warm-up is the time to merely loosen up and focus in. The movement will help to increase blood flow to the working muscles to provide oxygen for energy production and will enhance the elasticity of the tendons and connective tissues for greater ease of motion. Focusing on deep, full breathing and the sensations of your movements will help to create the body-mind connection—the mental concentration on your exercise. The cardiorespiratory system will gradually increase heart rate and blood pressure to accommodate the increased demand for oxygen from the muscles. Beginning your exercise too fast will overwhelm the body's systems. They will not be able to meet the rapid increase in demand, and you will fatigue quickly, possibly experience cramping or a "stitch," and feel emotionally and physically demotivated. You may end up shortening your workout as a result.

The session should end with a cool-down much like the warm-up to help the body's systems gradually return to rest and release the muscle tension that has built up during the activity. Final stretches during a cool-down should be a bit more advanced and static, held for 30 to 40 seconds. Focus primarily on those major muscle groups you used in your exercise. Perform muscle-specific, advanced stretches in order to take advantage of the warm body temperature, which allows greater stretching. Deeper stretching will effect a more permanent increase in the range of motion around the joint for greater flexibility. If you are planning to do some strength training during a particular workout session, you should wait to do your more intense or final stretching until after you have performed the muscle-conditioning exercises.

Monitoring Your Exercise Intensity

It is important to monitor your exercise intensity, so that you are exercising safely and effectively. Our cardiorespiratory system can function aerobically or anaerobically. Aerobic performance is stimulated by a moderate level of exercise intensity and causes the body to use oxygen to burn primarily fat for fuel. The anaerobic system, which is stimulated by a higher level of exercise intensity, does not use oxygen like the aerobic system and burns primarily body sugars stored in the muscle for fuel. Both systems are functioning when we exercise, but our exercise intensity level will determine which one is dominantly used. To enhance our aerobic conditioning, we need to continue to challenge our capacity by pushing to the *anaerobic threshold,* that is, working at more intense aerobic levels and pushing our aerobic capacity higher into anaerobic intensities.

How hard you exercise, or rather, at what level of intensity you work out; depends not only on how fit you are but also on your goals. Monitor yourself when exercising to ensure that you are working at the appropriate level of intensity. It is important that you are not overworking and causing yourself excess stress and injury. Make certain that you are not working at a level below that sufficient for conditioning. If you are focused on cardiorespiratory fitness, general health, and weight loss, it is best to exercise at a more moderate or *aerobic* level of intensity. A beginning rugged walker whose goal is to get into a regular exercise program to lose weight and become fit will begin a moderate program and may walk one or two miles three times a week at 3.5 to 4.0 miles per hour at an intensity, or target heart rate (THR), of 50 to 70 percent of MHR. In contrast, an advanced exerciser who is looking for a more challenging cross-training activity may work out more anaerobically or at a very high intensity and may walk five miles five to six times per week at 5.5 to 6.0 miles per hour at an intensity of 80 percent to 90 percent of MHR. Each exerciser wants to improve his or her fitness or aerobic level, which requires exercising at levels that challenge the anaerobic system. This may be accomplished by exercising more intensely in short, high-intensity bursts (for example, sprinting), which will utilize more of the *anaerobic* energy system.

In the rugged walker program you will perform interval training, which involves short intervals of anaerobic intensity interspersed between longer intervals of more moderate or aerobic-intensity walking. Your exercise intensity while rugged-walking can be affected by your speed, the ruggedness of the terrain, and the difficulty of the drills you perform. To be aware of whether you are exercising at the appropriate level of intensity—aerobically or anaerobically—you should monitor your exercise intensity. The two most recommended ways for monitoring your exercise intensity are THR and the rating of perceived exertion (RPE). Try them both then choose the one that feels more comfortable and gives you more information.

Target Heart Rate According to ACSM guidelines, for conditioning to occur, a target heart rate (THR) of 50 percent to 90 percent of your maximum heart rate (MHR) must be maintained for 20 minutes or more during each workout. To calculate your THR, multiply your MHR by the desired level of intensity (60 percent, for example). The most common formula used to first determine a rough estimate of your MHR is to subtract your age from the number 220. For a 40-year-old person, MHR would be 220 – 40 = 180 beats per minute. The THR then would be 180 x 0.60 (60 percent) = 108 beats per minute.

While you are exercising, you should take your pulse at least once during the time you feel you are at your THR, or in the steady level of intensity of your workout. Your pulse can be taken at your wrist (radial) or on the side of your neck (carotid—be sure not to press too hard here). Take your pulse for a 15 second count and then multiply by 4 to get beats per minute. Because you are taking your pulse while exercising, there will be some inaccuracy because of difficulty in your ability and sensitivity in finding your pulse while moving. Therefore, allow a THR range—a few beats above or below your THR—to be the measure of your intensity.

Calculating Your THR

Find your MHR:

220 – your age _____ = _____ (your MHR)

Find your THR:

Your MHR _____ x your desired level of intensity (50 percent for low intensity to 90 percent for high intensity) _____ = _____ (your THR)

Resting Heart Rate Resting heart rate (RHR) is not a direct measurement of exercise intensity, but it relates to MHR and THR. As you become more conditioned, your cardiorespiratory system becomes more efficient and your RHR may decrease. This may have some effect on your THR. RHR therefore can be a helpful indicator of cardiorespiratory conditioning. It is best to take your RHR before getting out of bed in the morning. As soon as you wake, take your neck or wrist pulse for one minute. The number of beats is your RHR. Find your average RHR by taking it for three days at least once a month, and be sure to use the same method each time.

Rating of Perceived Exertion The rating of perceived exertion (RPE) was designed to help you rate the intensity level during your workout by assessing your perceived levels of intensity, or how hard you feel you are working. This rating is a subjective judgment of your physiological functions—breathing, sweating, body temperature, muscular sensations, and so on—and has been shown to correlate closely to your heart rate. I recommend using RPE over THR because it evaluates your level of intensity according to how you feel and gives you feedback about your body and its overall responses than focusing just on heart rate. Therefore, you will have more control over your workout. RPE also has the advantage of being less disruptive to your workout because you are not struggling to find a pulse, and therefore it may possibly be more accurate.

To assess your perceived exertion, use the Borg scale (see figure 2.3) and follow the steps below.

1. Ask yourself: how hard do I feel I am exercising? Answer the question quickly without thinking about it too much.
   a. Breathing is an excellent indication of intensity. If you can speak very easily and do not feel that your breathing has

increased, then pick up the pace. If you cannot talk at all easily, you are working at an anaerobic level. This may be what you want during an intense interval; however if you are in a moderate interval, you may want to slow down. Remember to breathe deeply, evenly, and at a rate that is most comfortable.

b. Consider how your body feels: is it getting warm? Are you sweating (do you need to take your sweatshirt off)? Are your muscles feeling worked, possibly fatiguing, or are they feeling little sensation? For example, during high-intensity exercise you should feel rather warm and break a sweat, and you should feel a sensation of fatigue beginning to build in your muscles.

2. During the aerobic or recovery walking intervals, you should answer "somewhat hard," or 13 to 14 on the Borg scale, and "hard," or 15 on the Borg scale, during the anaerobic or high-intensity intervals.

3. If your response is "very light" (about 9 or below on the scale) or "very hard" (about 17 or above) adjust your workout intensity by increasing or decreasing, respectively, some of the following variables:

a. your speed

b. the arm pump (see chapter 3)

c. the terrain (e.g., hill climbing)

d. the number of intervals

e. the length of the interval

f. the degree of intensity of the terrain drills

g. the number of terrain drills

Note: A high- or anaerobic-intensity drill may involve speed walking or terrain drills or both and requires a level of effort at an intensity of "hard" to "very hard" on the Borg scale. The intensity of the drill can be increased or decreased depending on the speed and range of motion with which you perform the movement. Using more muscle power (*mind in the muscle* and *activated position,* discussed later in this chapter) than momentum will increase the intensity of your work (for example, large, deep lunges rather than small, shallow lunges). Also, activating the upper body by using the arms effectively increases the power of your work. The intensity of the drills can be affected by exercising on various terrains: uphill, downhill, paved road, dirt path. Keep in mind that you want to work "hard" (a level of 15 on the Borg scale) during your high-intensity intervals, but you also want to make sure you are not working "too hard" (a rating of 18+ on the scale). This level of intensity may be unsafe and is probably not fun.

6	**No exertion at all**
7	**Extremely light**
8	
9	**Very light**
10	
11	**Light**
12	
13	**Somewhat hard**
14	
15	**Hard**
16	
17	**Very hard**
18	
19	**Extremely hard**
20	**Maximal exertion**

The RPE scale, i.e., the 15-grade scale for ratings. Reprinted from Borg 1985.

Body-Mind Exercise Concepts

Mental focus and concentration are often important to doing something well. An understanding of body-mind concepts, which deal with the link between your mental focus and physical experience, will help make your rugged walk more effective and enjoyable. Often you get distracted from your exercise by thoughts of things you need to do later or what you did earlier rather than staying aware of what is happening in the present moment—staying aware of your body and your exercise. Working on being more present-minded, keeping your concentration on what you are doing by focusing on the body-mind connection, will ensure safe and effective exercise and teach you the practice of being more present in your life as well.

There are four body-mind concepts, the first of which, *reciprocating influences,* provides the basis for the other three. The concept of *reciprocating influences* is based on the understanding that you experience life not only physically, but mentally and spiritually as well, that there are intimate relationships between your body and mind, and that your body and mind reciprocally influence each other. This concept, along with three others, *neutral spine/neutral mind, mind in the muscle,* and *activated position*, help to articulate an understanding of the body-mind connection.

Reciprocating Influences

All life's experiences are experienced and manifested in the body. What you feel mentally and emotionally influences you physically—influences your body's health as well as its performance. Your body's health and performance reciprocate, influencing what you feel mentally and emotionally. This concept becomes more clear when we talk about posture, for example. How you feel emotionally causes you to posture yourself, or hold and move your body, a certain way. When you feel demotivated and sad, you slouch. How you posture yourself influences you to have certain feelings. When you slouch you may find you feel demotivated, sad, and withdrawn. Standing tall helps you feel confident and energized. Have you ever noticed how it makes you feel when you smile? Even when you are feeling down, the act of smiling can make you feel happier.

What is exciting about *reciprocating influences* is that by working with the body, your physical self, such as by exercising, eating well, or relaxing, you help your emotional self: you feel happier and more peaceful. By working with your emotional or spiritual self, such as by meditation, you help your physical self. Your body becomes more healthy and fit. *Reciprocating influences* are explored in greater depth in chapter 8 in a discussion concerning the negative effects of emotional stress on our physical well-being.

Neutral Spine/Neutral Mind

In order for exercise to be safe and effective, proper body alignment and attention to good technique are essential. Proper body alignment begins with a *neutral spine,* while attention to good technique begins with a *neutral mind. Neutral spine* is a position of balance: aligning the spine over the base of stability and therefore supporting the natural curves of the back; and keeping the curves of the back in the neutral position. This helps minimize the pull of gravity by enhancing the stability of the vertebral column and therefore significantly enhances shock absorption. *Neutral spine* allows the energy of the body to flow freely, helping you to feel energized, tall, and light. When you are out of alignment, gravity is believed to have a much greater impact on your body than when you are balanced. Misalignment pulls you downward, draining energy out of your body and making you feel physically and emotionally very tired and heavy. *Neutral spine* is important for avoiding muscular fatigue; soreness of the neck, back, and hips; and impingement of the vertebral disks. Chapter 3 presents more details about *neutral spine,* as well as exercises to help you achieve it.

Just as *neutral spine* is extremely important to performance and safety, so is *neutral mind.* The mind can be pushed out of balance when it is stressed by thoughts of worry and regret. Regrets of the past or worries of the future keep you from enjoying the present moment. When you are not present in the moment you are out of balance: you are not in touch with or aware of what you are actually experiencing. Exercising under emotional stress can significantly distract you from concentrating on what you are doing and how well you are doing it. This may lead to ineffectiveness and injury.

By practicing *neutral mind* while exercising, you stay more focused on your body and therefore more focused in the present

moment. Your work becomes more effective, safe, and most especially, enjoyable. To help you practice *neutral mind* and keep your
focus on your body, concentrate on your breathing. The breath is
the bridge connecting the mind with the body. This body-mind connection helps you to sense your body with greater awareness.

Your breathing is most effective when it is full and even. It may
be helpful to match the rhythm of your breathing to the rhythm
of your exercise. For example, when you are exercising aerobically—running or walking—your breathing will increase naturally.
Pay attention to your breathing rhythm and you may notice that
it is half the tempo of your walking or running pace. In strength
training it may be helpful to match your breathing rhythm exactly to the tempo of the exercise. For example, exhale when you ini-
tiate exertion in an exercise (e.g., lifting a weight), and inhale
when you release the exertion (lowering the weight). Check to
see, however, that each breath is full and deep in the chest and
belly rather than shallow or high in the chest. Be certain not to
force your breathing, as this will only build tension in the chest
and a general sense of stress. Chapter 8 presents further details
about how to stay more present-minded, or in *neutral mind*.

Mind in the Muscle

Comprehension and concentration are very important for exercising well. It may seem obvious to say that you should know
which exercises are working which muscles. However, sometimes
you perform exercises without really focusing your attention on
or comprehending the specific goal of the exercise. When you are
not focused, your effort often may be lazy, inappropriate, and
unsafe. Understanding the exercise completely will give you mental stimulation and the opportunity to perform the exercise cor-
rectly and with good energy. By concentrating, you make certain
that you are getting the most out of each exercise and not predis-
posing yourself to injury. It is important for you to have your *mind
in the muscle* when exercising.

Achieving *mind in the muscle,* or mental focus, can be accomplished by practicing paying attention to what you are doing and
how your muscle feels doing it. In this way you tie or connect the
sensation in your muscle with the goal or focus in your mind.

◆ Balancing on a rock requires neutral spine/neutral mind, mind in the muscle, and activated position.

Practice this technique when you are rugged walking. For example, focus on feeling your quadriceps, or thigh muscles, contracting and releasing as you hike up the hill.

Activated Position

Activated position concerns potential energy and the "ready" position. The ready position of the mind is *mind in the muscle*. *Activated position* is the ready position of the body. What this means is that just before you perform an exercise movement, activate, or create a slight energy, and cause some tension and contraction, or "ready energy," in the muscles. Hold this energy (as in an isometric contraction) during and between repetitions, or isotonic contractions, of an exercise. For example, you are encouraged to activate or energize your whole body to hold proper body alignment during exercise. Maintaining *activated position* during exercise ensures effective performance and safety.

Maintaining *activated position* takes *mind in the muscle*—your mind constantly reminding your body to maintain the energy of the ready position, to stay activated, and sensing this energy in your body. When rugged-walking, you are focused on holding proper body alignment so you are ready to execute a lunge or leap safely and effectively. In the next chapter we look at the importance of proper body alignment for rugged walking.

Walking Posture

Good posture is important for safe, effective, and comfortable rugged walking. People have long thought posture to mean a static position: how we stand and how we sit. Posture is not static, but rather the very dynamic, constantly changing condition of our body achieving balance. Rugged walking is an excellent way to enhance your balance and strengthen your posture. When we walk, we are actually moving rhythmically through a series of postures, constantly working with our sense of balance. How we achieve this balance affects the biomechanics of and therefore the efficiency of our walking: our stride technique. It is important therefore that you train and exercise in ways to enhance good posture. And it is important to begin this training with an understanding of your posture, particularly where it may be weak. Weaknesses you have may be aggravated by rugged walking if you do not take the time to understand and begin to correct your postural imbalances.

Many physical discomforts and injuries such as back pain, neck and shoulder tension, hip and knee soreness, and foot ailments may occur as a result of poor posture and unsafe body mechanics. Statistics show that back pain is the second leading cause of missed work in the United States and costs billions of dollars in health care annually. Four out of five Americans will experience serious back pain at some point in their lives, and this will greatly compromise the quality of their lives. The exact cause of back pain has long been a mystery. Is it physical? Is it psychological? Research and my personal opinion suggest that it is a combination of both. We know about *reciprocating influences,* so it is important to condition both our bodies and our minds to maintain balance and establish a healthy posture.

Achieving Balance of Body and Mind

Posture is a body-mind process, a *sense*-ational experience. We care about good posture because we care about moving easily, and looking and feeling sensational. Posture is not only about viewing how the body looks from the outside, as we typically do. More important, posture is also about viewing the body from within, or sensing how we feel, both physically and emotionally. Our posture is the physical reflection of our emotional relationship with our body: our self-image and our self-esteem. Our posture is the physical reflection of our attitude about life. It is a reflection of how we feel about ourselves in relation to the world around us. Our posture reflects how we sense the world and how we feel the world senses us. When we are out of sorts, emotionally unbalanced, we eventually feel it physically. This causes poor posture. Healthy posture is a sense-ational experience of achieving balance: balance of body and balance of mind.

The body-mind concepts related to posture describe posture as the positioning of the body in response to the *reciprocating influences* between our physical and mental selves, the sensations that occur between how we feel and how we move. What we are thinking and how we are feeling about ourselves, our "inner posture," significantly affect how we posture our physical self, or "outer posture." And our outer posture—how fit, healthy, and balanced our body is—reciprocates and influences our inner posture. Our posture is a result of conditioning to these reciprocating influences, and over time our body will maintain a certain alignment or posture. Take a moment to watch the postures of people you know and then think about their personalities. A confident person often has a very erect and open posture because he or she "approaches" life. A shy person often has a more slouched posture because he or she "withdraws" from life. A rugged walker conditions toward a balanced, open posture.

Posture as a Function of Balance and Energy

Your posture is a function of both your physical balance—your strength and flexibility—and your emotional balance—your disposition. Physical balance is achieved when your body, particularly your skeletal system, is aligned so that the pull of gravity on the body is minimized. The body works with gravity in the sense

◆ Rugged walking practices achieving balance of body and mind—good posture.

that it needs to find balance against gravity or it will fall down. The balanced position is when the weight or center of gravity of your body is directly over the center of its base of stability. This results in gravity pulling evenly on all parts of your body, therefore minimizing the general effect of gravity.

Mental and emotional balance is achieved by finding the center or balance point in your perspective. We will always have stressful thoughts, or worries, but by changing our perspective they may become less so. We may not be thrown off-balance emotionally so easily the next time something stressful happens. Mental balance comes from taking the time to relax and meditate. This process discussed in chapter 8 helps reduce stress and heightens our self-awareness and self-acceptance. This enhances our perspective and increases our focus or concentration on the experience of the present moment. This is mental balance. When your mind is in the present moment, it is more relaxed and more focused on your body and what it is experiencing, ensuring that you are exercising effectively and safely. As your mind becomes more relaxed, your body feels more freedom to move, giving more rhythm, grace, fluidity, and balance to your posture.

Posture also involves the flow of energy through your body and the interaction of your body's energy with the energies of the Earth. Dance can teach you much about this relationship because dance is the flow of energy. This flow of energy comes from your spirit and moves through your body. This energy interacts with the gravitational energy of the Earth in an effort to establish balance in movement. I liken the sensations you experience in dancing to what you feel when you are walking. Like dancing, walking is the process of working with the flow of energy through your body to find balance in movement, to find your walking posture. Dance is also a body-mind experience as it is the expression of the intimate connections between your body and your mind. Dance is a training technique that provides you the opportunity of bringing all aspects of your physical fitness—endurance, strength, power, flexibility, speed—as well as your mental and spiritual fitness—focus and expression—into play to establish balance. So is rugged walking. In rugged walking, you need to constantly adjust your body's balance by working your strength, flexibility, and power to move easily and safely over the rugged terrain. As in dance, the way you move across the rugged terrain reciprocates with the way you feel emotionally. It is wonderful to feel powerful at times climbing up a steep cliff and graceful at other times leaping over mud gullies.

Postural Analysis and Training

The first step in achieving healthy posture is through postural analysis: evaluating the curves of the spine and the body's alignment. The results of this analysis help determine which muscular strength and flexibility exercises are best to correct any weaknesses or imbalances. Muscular conditioning promotes the strength and endurance needed to hold balanced alignment. Flexibility conditioning enhances range of motion around your joints to allow the body free movement to assume balanced alignment. Flexibility and muscle conditioning exercises are presented in chapters 4 and 5, respectively. The concepts of *lift* and rhythm, taken from dance technique (see page 46) are very effective in helping you feel the sense-ational experience of posture, or rather the sensation of energy in helping to maintain healthy posture.

Neutral Spine

Postural analysis is based on the concept of neutral spine. Neutral spine is extremely important for establishing balance, providing good shock absorption to the body and avoiding injury. As explained in chapter 2, neutral spine results when the curves of your spine, and therefore the weight of your body, are balanced over the center of your base of stability. Your base of stability is established by the placement of your feet: having your feet close together makes your base smaller, while placing them farther apart makes your base larger. When you achieve neutral spine, the curves of your back are supported so that the back does not excessively arch or round. This position requires the pelvic girdle (your hipbones) to be held upright so the tailbone is neither pointed backward excessively (causing the lower back to arch) nor excessively tucked under (causing the lower back to flatten and the upper back to round).

If your back is abnormally arched or rounded, part of your spine is out of alignment and you are less balanced. If you are out of balance, the pull of gravity has a greater effect on your body. To resist falling, you adjust your balance by placing other body parts out of alignment to compensate for the initial imbalance, and this creates greater imbalance. Being out of balance or out of neutral spine has a significant influence on how your body absorbs impact when you walk, run, jump, and so on. Research has shown that when you are out of balance, the pull of gravity may have as much as 15 times greater effect on your body. Therefore, poor posture dramatically increases the wear and tear on your joints, increasing degeneration, aging, and the likelihood of injury.

Poor posture often manifests as lordosis (arched or hyperextended lower back) or kyphosis (rounding forward of the shoulders and hyperextension of the neck). These deviations often result from muscular imbalance and inflexibility, poor postural habits, or improper footwear. As a result of maintaining poor posture, muscles around the joints become imbalanced; some muscles become very tight while others are overstretched. Tight muscles shorten the range of motion around the joints. This limits your freedom of movement and makes you feel stiff. Overstretched

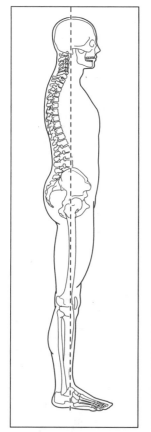 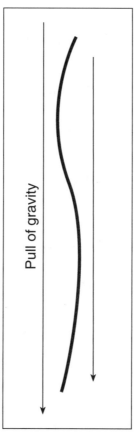 

Pull of gravity

◆ Neutral spine—the curves of your back are not excessively arched or rounded, and you are balanced over your base of stability.

muscles are muscles whose tendons and ligaments have become so permanently stretched that they provide little support around the joint. Imbalanced muscles, whether overstretched or too tight, are unable to provide support and stability to maintain a balanced body and therefore predispose you to injury.

Lordosis is usually a result of weak abdominals and back muscles and very tight hip flexors (primarily the iliopsoas). Kyphosis often occurs as a result of tight chest muscles, weak upper back and shoulder muscles, and tight hamstrings. To avoid and correct these imbalances it is important to design a program of exercises that focuses on strengthening muscles such as the abdominals, back, and shoulder and increasing flexibility for the hip flexors, hamstrings, and chest.

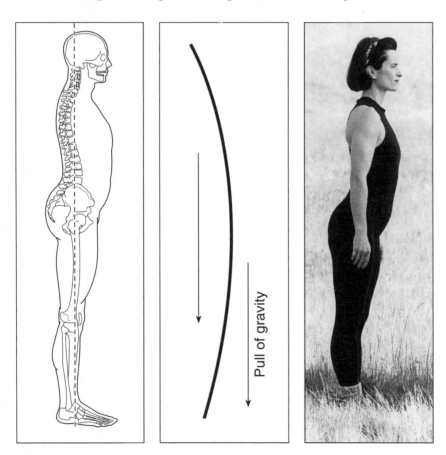

Pull of gravity

◆ Lordosis—excessive arching of the lower back. You are out of neutral balance over your base of stability.

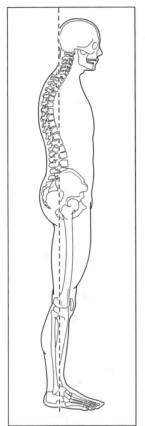 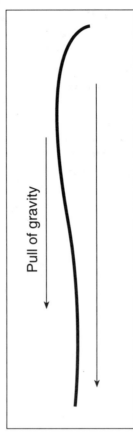 

◆ Kyphosis—excessive rounding of the upper back. You are out of neutral balance over your base of stability.

Postural Analysis

A postural analysis compares your posture with neutral spine. From this analysis you will become aware of the areas of your body that are out of alignment, and thus you will be able to design an appropriate exercise program to correct the imbalance and establish neutral spine.

Screening Checklist for Neutral Spine Following is a checklist for assessing your own posture. It is highly recommended that you see a physician if any of the following conditions appear severe or if you are feeling any physical discomfort during or after exercising.

While facing a mirror, ask yourself the following questions:

- Is your head held erect, neither tilted to the side nor dropping to the front or back?
- Are both shoulders the same height above the floor? If not, can you adjust yourself so they are balanced?
- Are both hipbones the same height above the floor? If not, can you adjust yourself so they are balanced?
- Are you bow-legged or knock-kneed? If severely so, you may need to be careful of injury.
- With your knees facing straight ahead, are your feet turned out at an angle of about 10 degrees? If they are overly turned out or turned in, you may need to be careful of injury.
- Does the weight of your body rest on the midstep of your feet, rather than on the inner or outer edges of your feet? If your arches are falling in, you may need an orthotic for support.

While standing in profile to the mirror, ask these questions:

- Is your head held upright, with the chin neither dropping nor jutting out and up? Your chin should be held horizontal, parallel to the floor.
- Are your shoulders rounded? They should be held open and aligned with your hipbones (up the side of your body).
- Is your upper back arching? It should be flat, not rounded or arched.
- Is the curvature of your lower back gentle rather than severe? Is it arched? Completely flat?
- Are your abdominals held in rather than relaxed and sticking out?
- Are the lower parts of your legs aligned under the thighs and the knees, or are they hyperextended (pushed back at the knee)?

Establishing Neutral Spine

The following steps will help you establish neutral spine. Work with these often so that you practice feeling the sensations of neutral spine and therefore can maintain it during all exercise.

1. Place feet about hip-width apart (to establish a good base of stability).

2. Adjust your body so that you feel that your weight is over the center of this base. Your weight should be centered between your feet. Your body should lean slightly forward from the ankle so your weight is over the instep of your feet rather than leaning back in your heels. Imagine looking at a picture of yourself from the side and drawing a line from the crown of your head to your heel. The line should indicate that your body is leaning slightly forward at the ankle.

3. Create a sense of energy or lift (see page 46 for details). Compress the abdominal wall toward the spine. Lengthen your spine by feeling your tailbone tip down (pointing your tailbone toward the floor) to bring your hipbones upright (in front). This will somewhat flatten the curve in your lower back, but be careful not to tuck the tailbone under so far that you completely flatten out the lower back.

4. Continue to practice the sensation of lift. Your chest should be lifted and open so that the shoulders do not round forward. Use a slight contraction in your upper back (squeezing your shoulder blades together), and be sure to relax your shoulders. Be careful not to arch the upper back. To avoid arching, as you lift the upper body, feel the sternum (breastbone) and ribs pull slightly downward and into your compressed abdominals. This is a very subtle adjustment but one that is very important. It greatly enhances your breathing capacity. When your upper back is arched or your shoulders rounded forward, your breathing capacity is much more shallow.

5. Feel both shoulders and both hipbones balanced equidistant from the floor.

6. Lift the head and neck by lifting up through the crown of your head so the neck feels as long as possible. The chin is held horizontal, neither tucked way in nor jutting way out. Imagine that your head is balanced at the top of your neck and that you are hanging like a puppet on a string. The string is attached to the back of a crown on the top of your head that connects through your head to the first vertebra of your neck.

Fitness Training for Healthy Posture

Since you are trying to establish balance in your body, it is very important that your exercise program provide balance in its training techniques. The program should be designed so that you strengthen and stretch muscles that are agonist-antagonist pairs (muscles that work opposite each other on each side of the joint). All day long your body is working to resist the pull of gravity, therefore maintaining good posture takes muscular strength and endurance. Strength training significantly improves your posture, which greatly reduces the risk of injury and enhances the effectiveness of exercising. Conditioning the upper body is important for maintaining a neutral spine. The upper back and shoulder muscles prevent your shoulders from rounding forward and dropping in at your chest. The latissimus dorsi, the large muscle of the middle and lower back, complements the abdominals to help stabilize your torso. It is also important to condition the lower body to maintain healthy posture because hip and thigh muscles are involved with the stability of the pelvic girdle. If your hip and thigh muscles are weak, your pelvis is less stable, resulting in aggravation to the back. Chapter 5 provides descriptions of strength-training exercises designed to improve posture.

Flexibility is also very important in our ability to maintain a healthy posture and avoid injury. We become very inflexible when we are experiencing muscular imbalance. Therefore, not only is it important that we strengthen the muscles that are weak and overstretched, it is just as critical that we stretch those muscles (or rather their tendons and ligaments) that are very tight. Also, be sure to maintain the flexibility in the other muscles as well. Most of us have tight chest muscles because we let our shoulders round forward, tight lower backs because we have weak abdominals that provide so little support we let our backs arch forward, and tight hamstrings and quadriceps because we do a lot of sitting in our lives. Therefore we need to do flexibility training to help these muscle groups loosen up. Chapter 4 presents flexibility exercises that are best for rugged walkers and great for everyone, whether rugged walker or not.

Dance Concepts for Rugged Walking

Training for a healthy walking posture can be significantly improved by practicing a technique borrowed from dance training called *lift*. Lift explores how to use the energy flow of your body so that you move gracefully and efficiently. In dance you learn to draw the energies from the earth up through your body to help you feel lifted and light, both physically and mentally. This has a direct effect on how you move. You feel lighter so you move more lightly. You do not feel as much impact as you walk.

Lift uses gravity to create oppositional forces within your body to enhance a more balanced and energized posture. As gravity pulls downward, you resist against that energy by pushing up or lifting up (lengthening) through your spine. You use your abdominals and upper body to create the energy of lift. Compressing in and lifting up the abdominals creates a sensation of support, or lift, to the spine. Holding your chest high (lifting up at your sternum) and open, which keeps your shoulders from rolling forward and your chest from dropping down, creates a strong sensation of lift in the upper body. Think of how a dancer holds his or her body. Dancers look long and lifted through their torso because they are using their abdominals and their upper body to create lift: ease and grace of movement.

When you are experiencing poor posture, you are not applying lift. Your body is out of balance. The energy flow through the body is blocked by the imbalance and thus causes you to be more heavy, both physically and mentally. No matter whether you are sitting or walking, you can always practice lift by sensing whether or not you feel light or heavy. It is quite simple really. If you feel heavy, create lift in your body until you feel light. Rugged walking is an ideal activity during which to practice lift.

Rhythm is another concept of dance that is important to consider with respect to posture. Rhythm is merely the tempo with which you move through your different postures when you are exercising. When your body finds a cadence or rhythm as you exercise, it experiences freedom, ease, and efficiency of movement. It finds the rhythm of establishing and reestablishing balance. Allow yourself to become aware of the rhythm of your rugged walk, and focus on the sensations you are experiencing. Rugged walking can significantly improve your sense of rhythm. As you walk, focus on the cadence of your feet and the tempo of your arms. Notice how your body feels with each step. Do you feel balanced? This rhythm will significantly help you feel "in the flow" of your walking technique. The next section on walking posture gives further details on walking in the flow.

Walking Posture and Stride Techniques

Believe it or not, there is more to walking than just walking. When it comes to achieving the fitness benefits you desire, proper posture and stride technique make the difference. Your stride technique affects your ability to achieve the speed and power that are needed to make the workout more effective, challenging, and safe. Your walking posture affects your stride technique. *How* you walk can affect

- your ability to increase your speed and thus the intensity of the walk,
- the degree of muscle conditioning you experience,
- your posture,
- your risk of injury, and
- your overall enjoyment.

The techniques presented in the following pages have proven to be very successful in helping people improve their walking posture and therefore their stride technique. These techniques align your torso and center of gravity for efficient biomechanics and breathing. They work to support the natural curves of your back, which will help minimize impact to your joints and thus reduce structural stress. The walking posture technique presented here is similar to race walking, but differs in the hip rotation and heel strike. Unlike race walkers, rugged walkers do not use a hip rotation, nor do they emphasize striking the back edge of the heel and striding forward on a straight leg. These techniques are primarily for race training and may tend to cause hip discomfort and hyperextension of the knee.

The rugged walker technique focuses on pushing off the back leg, specifically off the ball of the foot, rather than reaching the striding leg forward. The push comes from using all the muscles of the back of the leg: calf, hamstrings, and especially the gluteals. The abdominals also play an important role in this push because they stabilize your torso so that the push forward from your legs is efficient and powerful. The abdominals are also critical in creating the sensation and energy of lift. This helps to maintain posture by keeping your body weight lifted and slightly more forward, rather than sitting back on your heels. Rugged walking also uses the arm pump significantly to stimulate the upper body, which helps to maintain the energy of lift and therefore proper walking posture. The power and swing of the arm pump help to drive your energy forward. The overall physical sensation of the rugged walker technique is one of walking tall with power: your whole body is lifted; your abdominals, gluteals, and upper-body muscles contract to lift you up; and you lean slightly ahead of your feet as your legs and arms pump strongly to drive you forward.

At first this technique may feel awkward as you learn the components. However, like any other sport, once you have mastered the technique, you will eventually find yourself in the magic sensation of the "flow," when your rugged walking feels almost effortless and your body floats over the terrain. When you're in the flow, you will feel light and energized and more inclined to leap and jump over the rugged terrain much as a deer does. This type of training is wonderful because its diversity is so fun and because it challenges so many more muscles and neuromuscular patterns than simply walking or running do. You will also feel mentally in the flow when you feel it physically. It feels quite wonderful to be exercising and then suddenly realize that you are in your stride— in the flow: your body moves strongly and you feel mentally clear and emotionally strong, happy, and able to solve any problem.

The following sections will help you learn the rugged walking technique and find the energy of flow physically and mentally.

Walking Tall

Walking tall focuses on lift and allows energy to flow freely through the body, which helps you feel lifted and light as you move across the Earth and through the pull of gravity. You will use this energy to give power and drive to your walk.

Walk tall by drawing energy upward through your spine and through the crown of your head. Remember the tips for keeping a neutral spine and for experiencing lift. You will feel a lengthening up along your spine and feel lifted, light, and balanced over the midstep of your stepping or supporting foot (which is the center of your base of stability). Be sure to lean forward from your ankle and not your waist. Keep your chin tucked in, your shoulders down and relaxed, and your chest open. However, be careful to avoid arching your upper back.

Your Base of Power

The abdominal wall is the most important muscle group that provides support for proper body alignment. By compressing the abdominal wall (your abdominal area from the bottom of your ribs down to your hip and pubic bones) toward your back, you keep your torso aligned and stable. The compression should be enough to feel your lower back supported, but not so much that you tuck your tailbone too far under and flatten out your lower back. Remember the natural curves of your back are important for shock absorption. The compressed abdominal wall is also significant in creating the energy of lift. Lift up your abdominals as you compress them in. The abdominal wall provides you with a base of resistance to push against, providing power to the arm pump (discussed a little later) and therefore more intensity to your walk. To sense what I mean, walk first with your abdominals relaxed. Then walk with your abdominals compressed. Feel the support? Using the abdominals in this way is an extremely effective way to condition them, and this technique will help them not only to become stronger but also to lie flat.

A good example of how important a stable torso is to providing power to your walking is demonstrated by decathlete Jackie Joyner Kersey. If you watch her running toward you, you notice that her torso is very stable, hardly twisting at all, and that her arms and legs are pumping with all the power she can muster. She uses her stable torso—stabilized by the compression of her abdominal wall—as her base of resistance to push against to powerfully pump her arms and legs. If her torso were not stabilized, it would twist as she pumps her arms and legs. This would allow some of the power of her pump to be wasted in the twisting action and therefore taken away from the forward direction. This would be a loss of efficiency in her running, and in your walking.

Stride

Think of very long legs: imagine that your legs are connected all the way up at your sternum. This will help you to feel the sensation of walking tall. With each stride, focus on pushing from the rear leg rather than reaching forward with the front leg. This will facilitate the forward motion and work the gluteals and hamstrings more effectively. Begin your stride by stepping on the pad of your heel with your toes pointing straight ahead. Next, transfer your body weight forward over the instep and ball of the striding foot. Roll through the foot and push off energetically from the ball of the foot. Focus on contracting the muscles of the back of your leg, particularly your gluteals, to feel a real energy to your push-off. Keep your knee relatively straight; however, avoid hyperextending the joint and stepping onto a stiff, locked leg. The striding foot should pass close to the support foot as you move. As your pace increases, gradually work toward walking on an imaginary straight line: step one foot almost directly in front of the other so that the arch or inside edges of your feet fall on that straight line.

The length of your stride may be the most important element of this technique. It should be comfortable and relatively short rather than long. Short strides are more effective than long strides in maintaining body alignment and increasing your speed. If your stride length is too long, you will feel as if your body weight is falling back into your heels. It will feel like you are pulling your body from behind rather than pushing it forward. As you increase your speed, your stride length should become shorter. See the section on speed later for more details in increasing your speed.

The Arm Pump

Pumping your arms helps to support balance, maintain body alignment, and provide power to your stride. It brings an important sensation of lift to the upper body. Experiment to feel the difference in your body when you walk with and without the arm pump. Keep the elbow bent 90 degrees and pump the arms slightly more forward than backward. The arms should pump in a powerful, relaxed, fluid large range of motion from the shoulder joint. The elbows should remain close to your body with the forearm passing slightly across the front of the torso toward the midline of the body, or belly button.

Speed

Speed is all in the arms. Use your arm pump as you would a metronome on a piano to set the tempo or pace of your walk. To increase speed, increase the tempo of your arms. It's that simple.

The speed and range of motion of the legs will follow. Focus on increasing the number of steps in sync with your arm tempo rather than increasing the length of your stride. Let your body fall forward into the rhythm of your new tempo.

Breathing

Breathe deeply and focus on feeling relaxed. Proper breathing is critical to efficient energy production as you exercise, and it is the single most effective way for you to relieve your physical and mental tension. In addition to supplying the needed oxygen, breathing also relieves the blood of carbon dioxide, a waste product that is produced when cells use oxygen.

Often we do not realize how inefficiently we are breathing. We have a tendency to take very shallow breaths, using only part of our thoracic (chest) cavity. Therefore, we actually need to learn to be better breathers. Take deeper breaths by using your diaphragm to draw the air down further into your belly; this will expand your chest cavity for greater capacity. Allow your breathing to be relaxed, full, and rhythmic. It is important not to force your breathing but to find a pattern of breathing that is comfortable. This will help to release tension while making you feel more energized. Focusing on your breath will help you focus in the present moment: on your body and on how you are exercising.

Uphill and Downhill

Walking uphill uses more of the muscles of the back of your leg (calf, hamstrings, and gluteals), whereas walking downhill uses more the front of the leg (the quadriceps). To walk uphill, lean the body into the hill and drive forward by pumping your arms and contracting the muscles on the back of your legs. Slightly lunge into your forward step. Your stride can be wide, as in lunging, or shorter for more speed, whichever is more comfortable. If you feel out of breath, it helps to turn around and walk uphill backward. This uses less muscle power and thus less energy. Be sure however not to stop completely to catch your breath. This may be dangerous to your safety. When we are exercising, our heart works hard to pump blood out to our extremities, and the contraction of the muscles in our arms and legs helps to push the blood back. If you stop exercising suddenly, the muscles in your legs are not helping to push the blood back. You have created an imbalance in your blood flow; the heart has less blood to push out and it is pushing against a lot of pressure: blood in the legs and arms. The blood will tend to pool in your extremities, and you could faint. Therefore, it is best to bring your tempo down and keep moving so your heart and blood flow have a chance to adjust. You will eventually regain your breath.

Walking downhill may feel a bit less stable than walking uphill. Be sure to check the terrain a bit more often for loose gravel or slippery mud. To walk downhill, slightly lean your body weight back into your heels. Control each step so that you resist the momentum that is created by the pull of gravity. You, rather than gravity, should control the rate of your descent. Your quadriceps, or thigh muscles, will be doing most of the work. Use the abdominal wall also to provide control and support to the lower back. If the terrain is slippery, muddy, or icy, do not lean back to prevent slipping. Walk more from midstep to toe rather than from heel to toe. Trust your body. It will tell you what to do.

Practicing Your Walking Posture

A great way to learn this walking technique is to practice one component of it at a time. Begin first by walking the way you normally walk, relaxed and easy. After a short distance, when you feel a bit warmed up, begin to *walk tall* by lengthening your spine and lifting up through the crown of your head. Lengthen your spine as you compress the abdominal wall, *your base of power,* for support to your torso. As you continue walking, next focus your attention on the *stride.* Remember to keep your strides shorter rather than longer so that your body weight is forward over your feet rather than falling behind into your heels.

Bring your attention to the *arm pump.* Bend your elbows 90 degrees and pump your arms easily, remembering to keep the elbows close to the body. Pump slightly more forward than backward. To increase your speed begin by pumping the arms a bit faster. The legs will follow. Last, but very important, give full attention to your *breathing.* It should be full, easy, and at a rhythm that is comfortable and consistent with your speed.

Flexibility for Rugged Walkers

Flexibility is very important in our ability to move easily and gracefully. It helps keep us young and vibrant. Flexibility is a significant factor in good posture and safe body mechanics. It helps us prevent injury by increasing the range of movement around our joints so that we can move freely. If we have limited flexibility, we feel stiff and our range of motion, our ability to perform certain movements, is limited and our posture becomes imbalanced.

Flexibility training is a very essential component of a well-rounded health and fitness program. We often neglect flexibility training, and yet it may be the most important factor in our ability to continue to exercise and play sports, not to mention merely performing everyday activities with ease. It seems that many sports injuries, particularly when we are older, happen as a result of our inflexibility. Many physical discomforts such as back pain, neck tension, and soreness come from being inflexible. Our typical daily routine, particularly if we are engaged in a lot of office work, can lead to inflexibility because of the lack of movement. Our muscles become stiff and tight, making it harder and less safe to perform even simple tasks.

Stretching feels so good. It releases muscle tension, stiffness, and soreness. Beginning each day with stretching loosens you up, both physically and mentally. Performing flexibility exercises provides an excellent opportunity to work with the relationship between your body and your mind. The stretching technique involves working with deep, full breathing to induce the relaxation response both physically and mentally. As you breathe, bring your attention to the muscle you are stretching. This encourages the muscles to relax and release tension, allowing for a greater stretch. This release and stretch occur on both a physiological and psychological level. Physiologically, when you take a deep breath, the body's systems will instinctively calm down. Heart rate, blood pressure, and adrenaline output slow down. As the body calms down, the mind reciprocates to help ease mental activity. As your mind calms, the body calms further. This calmness and relaxation allows your muscle to stretch more. You feel more physically and emotionally flexible.

This chapter presents stretching exercises that are most commonly recommended by fitness professionals for flexibility training, as well as some variations on how to use these stretches in your natural environment to add diversity and fun to your rugged walking program. Also included are descriptions of modified tai chi exercises, which are designed to enhance your flexibility by improving your fluidity of movement and balance. Tai chi is also optimal for enhancing the body-mind connection because you perform these exercises with great focus on your breathing and the sense you have of your body's energy. These exercises also bring your attention to the nature around you and how you feel in relationship to it.

General Stretching Exercises

The following stretching exercises should be performed after you have exercised or at least taken a few minutes to warm up thoroughly. A nice, easy, brisk walk followed by a few rhythmic, gentle stretching movements would do well. After a warm-up the muscles and tendons will be warmer and thus more flexible. Before performing any stretch, check your body alignment and make sure it is balanced. Particularly if you are standing, you should check for good posture and hold a neutral spine. The stretches should be performed slowly and with a full range of motion. You may want to perform some of the stretches dynamically (moving slowly and rhythmically through the range of the stretch), which is best for warming up, or perform them as static stretches that should be held for 30 to 40 seconds for flexibility conditioning. Keep your attention on what you are feeling in the muscles as you stretch. The degree of stretch should create a large range of motion at the joint until you feel tension in the stretching muscle. It is important to stretch to the point of tension, but never to the point that you feel pain. Remember to use your breathing to assist in releasing the tightness. As you hold the stretch, you will feel the tension in the muscle build at first and then gradually ease. At this point, you may want to stretch a little farther to a new point of tension, which will be at a new range of motion.

◆ Chest ◆

major and minor pectorals

Standing in proper posture with your arms at your sides, bring your straight arms behind your back and clasp your hands. Keep your shoulders down and allow the arms to rotate outward at the shoulder and the shoulders to reach backward until you feel a stretch in the chest. For variation: While in this position, lift your hands further away from you to feel a deeper stretch in your chest and shoulders.

◆ Neck Flexions ◆

neck, shoulders, back: trapezius, erector spinae, deltoids

Standing in proper posture, tip your head to the left by tipping your left ear to your left shoulder so that your chin is still facing front. As you hold this stretch, for 30 seconds or so, press your left shoulder down. Lift your head back up to the center. Next tip your head, ear to the right shoulder. Hold the stretch for 30 seconds, and press your left shoulder down. Return to the center. Next tip your chin to your chest. Hold the stretch for 30 seconds, and press both shoulders down. For variation: You may want to also perform this stretch dynamically. Tip your left ear to your left shoulder, then roll your chin to the chest and come up center. Then repeat this to the right side. It is not recommended that you roll your head to the back, as this may cause stress to your neck's vertebrae.

◆ Shoulder Raises and Depressions ◆

neck, shoulder, torso: trapezius, latissimus dorsi, intercostals

Standing in proper posture, raise your shoulders up to your ears as much as possible. Feel the sides of your torso stretch. Hold the stretch, and then tip very slightly to the left side. Feel a deeper stretch on the right side. Tip to the right side. After returning to the center, depress both shoulders as much as possible. Feel the stretch across the neck and shoulders. For variation: You may want to raise and lower your shoulders in a slow rhythm through the full range of motion.

◆ Shoulder Rolls ◆

shoulders, upper back, chest: trapezius, latissimus dorsi, pectorals

Standing in proper posture, roll your shoulders very slowly in big circles toward the back, and then reverse the circle toward the front. The bigger the circle, the deeper the stretch in the chest, upper back, and shoulders.

◆ Torso Reach ◆

sides of the torso: obliques, latissimus dorsi, intercostals

Standing in proper posture, reach your left arm up overhead, and place your right hand on your left hip. Reach the arm overhead up toward the sky, and allow your torso to stretch with the reach; tip very slightly into your reach, toward your right side. Repeat to the other side.

◆ Upper-Back Stretch ◆

posterior deltoid, rhomboids, trapezius

Standing in proper posture, bring both arms up in front and clasp your hands. Round your upper back, allowing your chin to drop toward your chest, and push your arms forward—into your hands— until you feel a stretch in your upper back. For variation: While in this position, slightly raise your right shoulder and feel the stretch deepen on the right side of your torso. Repeat this on the left side.

◆ **Lower-Back Stretch** ◆

erector spinae, latissimus dorsi

Use the same position as in the upper-back stretch; however, allow yourself to curve your whole spine more by rounding your shoulders more and tucking your tailbone under until you feel a stretch in your lower back.

◆ Forward Lunge ◆

calf: gastrocnemius—straight leg, soleus—bent leg

Lunge forward on your left leg, while keeping your right leg straight in the back. Keep your left knee directly over the left heel. Keep your hips straight; avoid letting your right hip open up or lean backward. Pull your right hipbone gently forward so it is in line with your left hipbone. Keep your right heel on the ground and allow your right knee to be soft rather than stiff. Feel the stretch relatively high in the back of your calf. Next, bend your right knee a little bit more while keeping your heel on the ground and feel the stretch move lower and closer to your heel. Repeat on the other side.

◆ Forward Lunge With Pelvic Tilt ◆

thigh: hip flexors, quadriceps

Use the same position as in the preceding Forward Lunge. However, release the right heel from the ground and allow the right knee to be fully relaxed. Next, tuck your tailbone under. While holding this position, gently push your right thigh backward until you feel a stretch on the front of your right thigh and close up to your hip joint. The more you tip your tailbone under and press the right leg toward the back, the deeper you will feel the stretch. For a complementary variation, turn out your right knee before you tip the tailbone under. As you tip the tailbone under, you will feel a stretch come up more on the inside of the right thigh and close to the hip joint rather than on the front. Repeat for the other side.

◆ Forward Lunge With Torso Flexion ◆

thigh, hip, and calf: hamstrings, gluteals, gastrocnemius

Use the same position as for the Forward Lunge. Lean forward into a wall or some sort of support, or support your arms on your left, or front, leg. While compressing your abdominals to provide support to your lower back, tip your torso forward from the hip (avoid bending forward at the waist) over your left thigh. Feel the sensation of tipping your whole torso as one unit forward so that your tailbone tips up out back. It is important to keep your back straight. Hold your body weight on your arms, either on your thigh or against the wall. Feel the stretch in the hamstrings and the hip of your left leg and in the hamstrings and calf of your right leg. Repeat on the other side.

◆ Standing Hamstrings Stretch ◆

thigh, calf: hamstrings, gastrocnemius

Stand with your right leg out in front of you, and balance most of your weight on the left leg. Soften the left knee to a slight bend, dropping your hips lower to the ground. Flex your right foot so that you feel a stretch up the calf. Place both hands on the left thigh for support to your torso while you tip your whole torso forward from the hip. You may also place your hands on a rail for balance and support. Compress the abdominals to support the lower back. Feel the stretch work up the back of your leg. The further you tip forward, keeping your back straight, the more stretch you will feel.

◆ Plantar Flexion ◆

shin: tibialis

Stand with your right leg out in front of you, and balance most of your weight on the left leg. Hold on to a rail for balance. Point your right foot toward the ground. Feel the stretch in the front of your shin. This stretch may feel better with your shoe off because you will be able to point a little further. Also, it can be done very slowly in a rhythmic fashion (point, flex, point, flex, and so on). Repeat on the other leg. This stretch is particularly great after your speed-walking training.

◆ Quadriceps Stretch ◆

thigh, shin: quadriceps, hip flexors, tibialis

Standing in proper posture, bend your right knee and lift your right foot behind you and take it in your right hand. Keep your right hip from rising up—both your hipbones should be the same height from the ground—and compress your abdominals to support your lower back. Keep your right heel about three inches from your buttocks. Feel your quadriceps stretching by lengthening your thigh and reaching your knee toward the ground. Repeat on the other leg.

◆ Side Lunge ◆

inner thigh: adductors

Stand with your legs far apart, and lunge your right leg out to the right. Keep your knees facing front and make sure your right knee is over your ankle and heel rather than leaning out over your toes, which puts great pressure on the knee joint. Place both hands on the right thigh for support. Keep your torso standing upright and feel the stretch in your inner thighs. Also, for a deeper stretch, after you are in your lunge on the right side, try to slightly tip your right hip out to the right. Be sure to keep your tailbone down. Feel the stretch deepen in the inner thigh of your left leg. For variation: Bending your torso forward while lunging into your right leg will stretch your right hamstrings and advance the stretch on the inner thigh of the left leg. Repeat to the other side.

◆ Supine Torso Curl ◆

hips, back: gluteals, erector spinae

Lying on the ground, pull your knees to your chest with your right leg crossed over your left leg, and wrap your arms around your legs. Raise your head toward your chest, your forehead to your knees, and feel the stretch down your neck, the length of your back and in your right hip. Concentrate on bringing your tailbone off the ground and curling it toward your chest for a deeper stretch of your lower back. Repeat the stretch with your left leg crossed over your right leg.

Stretching With Nature

Nature provides a wonderful studio in which to stretch after your rugged walk. Look around and you are sure to find a tree, log, or rock to help you stretch. A tree's branch is a perfect ballet barre to stretch on or hang from for a full-body stretch. A log serves as a great bench to sit on and stretch hamstrings, lower back, and calves. If you are outdoors in the city, park benches, street curbs, and light poles serve just as well.

A series of stretching exercises designed specifically for rugged walking is presented here. Some of these stretches are essentially modifications of the general stretches given in the previous section. There are many more that you can modify and create to meet your own particular needs. Chest, upper back, lower back, hip flexors, gluteals, hamstrings, quadriceps, adductors, and calves are of particular focus in these rugged walker exercises because these are the primary movers in rugged walking.

◆ Hang Person ◆

shoulders, torso

Hang, like a rag doll, from a branch that is about arm's length overhead. Feel the lengthening of the whole body. Or use a branch that is lower, but bend your knees to pick up your feet so they are not touching the ground.

◆ Body Arch ◆

full-body stretch, front side

Stand under a branch that is about an arm's length above your head. Hold on to the branch tightly and keep your feet in the same spot while performing this stretch. Allow your body to arch back, leaning forward with your hips, so that your back and whole body is arching. Feel the stretch in the front of your body: hips, abdominals, chest, shoulders, and arms. Option: If the branch is about upper-back height, stand with your back to the branch, reach your arms overhead, and arch back over the branch.

◆ **Body Curl** ◆

full-body stretch, back side

This stretch is the reverse of the Body Arch. Hold tightly on to the branch with arms extended and allow your hips to pull backward and tuck your tailbone under (as in a pelvic tilt). Curl your whole body as you lean backward. Feel the stretch through the back of your body from your shoulders, down your back, and through your buttocks.

◆ Hang Body ◆
full-body stretch

Stand at a branch that is about waist level from the ground. Bend over the branch at the hips, letting your head, torso, arms, and legs hang loose.

◆ Log Leg Lunge ◆
hamstrings, gluteals, quadriceps, hip flexors

Face a log, large rock, or park bench, and lunge with your right leg on top of the log. Bend this knee so that it is directly aligned over the heel rather than leaning forward over the toes. Straighten the left leg while keeping your heel on the ground. Both knees and toes are facing straight ahead. Tip the torso forward over the right leg at the hips while keeping your back straight so that your tailbone is pointing directly out to the back. Feel the stretch in the hamstrings of the right leg and in the calf and hamstring of the left leg. Bring your torso back up to a vertical position, bend the knee of the back leg, and lower your body down a few inches. Feel the stretch in the hamstrings of the right leg (on the log) and in the hip flexor and quadriceps of the left leg. Repeat on the other side.

◆ Log Quadriceps Stretch ◆
quadriceps, hip flexors

Face away from the log, rock, or park bench, and place your right foot up behind you, resting the top of your shoe on the log. Stand close to the log so that your right thigh is close to and almost parallel to your left leg. Although this may feel impossible, try to tip your tailbone under, and feel the stretch in the front of the right hip. The tip or pelvic tuck is very subtle. Gently bend the left leg and feel the stretch in the right thigh deepen. If you now move a bit farther away from the log and allow the right leg to reach back while still trying to keep your tailbone down (not letting your hips tip backward and your lower back arch) the stretch will be more intense.

◆ Log Hamstrings and Calf Stretch ◆

calf, lower back, hip

Sit on a log, large rock, or park bench with your right leg in front of you with its calf resting on the log, knee slightly bent, and the left leg on the ground for balance. Flex your right ankle and reach for your foot while trying to maintain a flat back. If reaching for your foot is too difficult, reach toward your shin or knee. Feel the stretch through the lower back, hip, hamstrings, and calf. To feel more stretch in the hamstrings, bend your knee just a bit more and lean your torso further over your thigh while working to maintain a straight back.

◆ Log Inner-Thigh Stretch ◆

adductor

Stand with your right side to a log, place the right leg straight on top of the log, and let the calf rest on the log. You need to be far enough away from the log to feel a gentle stretch on the inner right thigh, but not so far away that it is difficult to stand up straight or that your hips are dramatically tilted. You should stand as tall and upright as possible. Compress your abdominals and then gently tip your hips away from the log; that is, tip your left hip out to the left. Feel the stretch become more intense in the inner right thigh. Repeat on the other side.

Tai Chi

Tai chi provides flexibility, balance, and fluidity training for the body, whose influence reciprocates with the mind, helping to keep you more mentally flexible and balanced. Modified tai chi exercises are included in the rugged walker workout for the primary purpose of strengthening the body-mind connection by heightening your awareness of the intimate relationship among the body, the mind, and the spirit. Tai chi also heightens your awareness of your intimate relationship with nature. Understanding and working with these relationships is critical to your well-being: your health, fitness, and happiness.

Tai chi movements help you concentrate on the sensations of the movements and waves of energy in your body, the body-mind connection. Tai chi focuses on teaching us awareness of this energy, which is the life force of nature within and around our body. The energies of our body and nature are very intimately connected. Take a moment to feel the sensations in your body when it is very gray and rainy out or when it is very sunny and crisp. Tai chi focuses on moving the energy and reawakening you to its life force, its healing, its balance, and its wholeness. Focus on your breath moving in and out of your belly and chest. Feel the sensations in your body as you perform these exercises. Time your breath with your movements so that you become fully focused on the body and its sensations.

You might say tai chi also has a very emotional, even spiritual, energy that encourages us to feel gratitude and humility for the beauty and bounty that nature bestows on us. We should have great respect for nature in all its glory and power. These exercises help to remind us not to take the Earth for granted, but to remember to find time to appreciate the nature around us. After all, we are intimately connected to it: we depend on it for our sustenance.

The following modified tai chi exercises are excellent for warm-up, cool-down, muscle conditioning, stretching, and stress reduction. If you perform them with ease and fullness, they loosen up the joints, release tension, and warm up the body. If they are performed with power and strength, they are very effective muscle-conditioning exercises. If they are performed with grace and fluidity, they are superb cool-down movements, releasing tension while enhancing flexibility. Once you have mastered these, you may want to make up your own. Be certain to pick a beautiful spot to perform these exercises.

◆ Nature Worship ◆

full body

This is a full-body stretch and is similar in movement and energy to yoga. It is a great stretch with which to begin and end your day or your stretching routine, as it stretches the whole body and brings your mind back into the present moment by focusing your attention on your breath. You will feel calmer, more in tune with yourself, and more in touch with nature.

You should feel very relaxed when performing this stretch. Take a deep, relaxed breath while getting ready to start.

1. Stand with your legs together, knees slightly bent, palms facing in and held at the belly (*a*). Circle the arms down, out to the sides, and up over head (*b*).

The palms meet overhead (*c*). Slowly bring the hands down the center of the body to return them to the belly (*d*).

2. As you circle the arms, slowly straighten the legs and bend them again as you bring the hands down to the belly.

3. These movements coincide with the timing of your breath. Inhale as you circle your arms up overhead. Exhale as the arms come from overhead to return to the belly.

4. Imagine as you circle the arms that your hands are gently scooping energy from the Earth, then up to and in from the heavens and bringing it back to the belly. Imagine you are releasing energy out from your belly to nature and bringing energy from nature back in.

5. Perform the same moves but reverse the arm circle. Inhale as you begin to reach the arms up the center of your body and over your head, and exhale as your circle your arms out from there and down your sides. Return your hands to your belly.

◆ **Picking Up Grass** ◆

gluteals, quadriceps, hamstrings, inner thigh

1. Stand with your legs slightly wider than hip distance apart, knees and toes facing straight ahead, palms facing the belly (*a*).
2. Raise your arms wide to the sides to shoulder height as you squat or bend in the knees, dropping the buttocks as if to sit down (keeping your weight in your heels) and allowing your torso to lean forward at the hip (keeping the back straight) (*b*). Look forward.

3. As you squat, drop your arms back down to scoop the hands toward each other in the grass, as if you are picking up grass (*c*).

4. As you begin to stand up, raise your arms up in front of your face, elbows extended and then lower slowly to finish with the hands in front of the belly (*d*). Contract the buttocks as you stand.

5. Draw the breath in as you bend, scoop, and raise the arms up. Exhale as you bring the hands back to the belly.

6. Repeat with the legs turned out (inner thigh emphasized).

◆ Push/Pull ◆

triceps, pectorals, biceps, upper back

1. Stand with your feet about hip-width apart and your knees and toes facing straight ahead. Slightly relax your knees so you feel the tailbone drop or tuck down toward the ground (feel as if there is a weight hanging from a string tied to your tailbone). Tighten your abdominals to provide support to your back and lengthen through the spine.

2. Raise your arms to your chest keeping your hands close to your body. Palms face your body and your elbows are lifted out to the side and shoulder height (*a*).

3. Rotate your palms outward, thumbs turning in to you and down to the ground, and *push* forward until your elbows are straight (*b*).

4. Rotate your palms toward your body and *pull* your hands into your chest. Pull your elbows slightly behind your torso, feeling a deep stretch in your chest and a contraction in your upper-back muscles.

5. Each time you push out, lower your arms a few inches so that as you pull them in they are close into your body a few inches lower than the pull before (*c*). Push and pull three times. On the third time, your hands should be in front of your belly (*d*). From there raise the elbows back up so that the hands are once again close to the body at chest height. As you raise your hands to your chest, keep them close to your body.

6. Exhale as you push, and inhale as you pull. Imagine that you are pushing away all the air in the world (and there is resistance because you are pushing a huge mass away) and that you are pulling all the air back to you (again with resistance, *mind in the muscle* and *activated position*).

7. On the third pull, inhale a longer breath as you raise the hands back up to the chest from the belly to begin the next sequence.

◆ Parting the Wild Horse's Mane ◆

internal and external shoulder and hip rotators

1. Stand with your feet slightly wider than hip's distance apart, knees and toes facing straight ahead, hands held one over the other in front of the belly, palms facing each other with the left palm facing up and the right palm facing down (*a*).

2. Slowly move the left arm, palm up, out away from you to the left side and turn your torso and hips to the left and toward the back so you can reach behind you (*b*). The right arm, palm down, extends out behind you (as you turn away from it). Your right arm is internally rotating at the shoulder. Allow your hips to rotate freely, letting the legs release and rotate too as you turn to the left.

3. Return to face front, switching hands so the right hand is on the bottom, left on the top, palms facing each other (*c*).

4. Reach the right hand away from the body, rotating right and twisting your torso toward the right. The left arm internally rotates while extending that arm out behind you (*d*).

5. Exhale as you extend your arms and rotate the torso toward the back. Inhale as you return facing front and your palms to the belly.

6. Imagine you are moving the energy away from the body as you turn and reach out, and returning it to the belly as you turn to face front and return the hands to the belly.

Note: As you extend the arms and rotate the torso to the back, allow your vision to see and your spirit to take in all that is around you.

◆ **Reaping** ◆

gluteals, quadriceps, hamstrings, upper arm, back

1. Stand with your legs wider than hip's distance apart, knees and toes facing forward. Arms are down at your sides.

2. Sway your body, right-left-right, and let your arms swing slightly side to side with your body (*a* and *b*). As you are swinging, move your arms as if you are reaping, sweeping things together on the ground with big movements to pick them up, although you are still standing. Reap in a rhythm of 1, 2, 3, 4: sway and swing your arms to the right on count 1, to the left on count 2, back to the right on count 3, then keep moving right and on the count of 4 lunge to the right and sweep your arms outward over your right lunging leg (*c*). Be sure to turn your head in the direction of your arms and look out as you reach the arms out right. Repeat this 1-2-3-4 rhythm and sequence to the other side.

3. Inhale as you are sweeping, reaping the energy in front of you on counts 1 and 2. Exhale on 3 and 4 as you lunge out to the side.

4. As you sway on 1, 2, and 3, imagine that you are reaping energy from around and within you and that as you lunge on 4 you are releasing that energy out to infinite space. Feel very light. Imagine that you are breathing this energy.

5. After you have done eight sets (eight patterns on each side), take out the reaping or sweeping section on counts 1, 2, and 3, and merely lunge side to side on the count of 1 and 2, right and left, as if you were speed skating, keeping the torso close to your thighs. Repeat 8-16 times.

6. From this deep right and left lunging, begin to lift the torso and to lunge less deeply so that the body is rising to an upright position. Now allow the body to sway side to side in a shallow lunge, and lift the left leg as you lunge to the right side. Repeat to the other side, lifting the right leg. Continue to do this as your lunges become more shallow and you become more erect, back straight. Now lift each leg straight out to the side while your arms reach out to the opposite side, keeping the supporting leg also relatively straight, but knees soft.

7. Bring the swaying into smaller movements. Stop lifting the legs. Bring your legs together and finish with a deep breath and full arm circle overhead.

◆ Flying and Soaring ◆

gluteals, hamstrings, anterior deltoid (upper arm), back

1. *Flying:* Stand with your legs about hip-width apart, knees and toes facing forward. Instead of going from side to side, as in Reaping, you are reaching front to back, as if you were cross-country skiing. Begin to swing your right arm forward and your left arm to the back (*a*). Swing the arms three times. Your feet and legs do not move. Hold on count 3, with the right arm in front at shoulder height. Holding on count 3, shift your weight to the left leg, lift your right leg to the back and bend or lunge on your left leg on count 4 (*b*). Then lower the right leg, and swing the left arm forward to repeat the pattern on the other side. Keep your feet on the ground, and swing the arms left-right-left on the count of 1, 2, 3. Hold the arms on count 3, shift your weight to your right leg, raise the left leg to the back on count 4, and bend into the right leg.

After you have practiced the movement a few times and feel comfortable with it, pick up the tempo. As you move into the lunge position, feel yourself reaching with your arms, lunging deeply, and reaching the leg out to the back so that you feel your whole body stretch. The rhythm is the same as that in Reaping. Repeat the sequence several times.

2. Inhale on counts 1 and 2. Exhale on counts 3 and 4.

3. *Soaring:* Change the rhythm from 1, 2, 3, 4 to 1 and 2. Alternate lunging right and lunging left. For the lunge right reach the left arm forward, lift the left leg, and lunge on your right leg (*c*). For the lunge left, reach the right arm forward, lift the right leg to the back, and lunge into your left leg (*d*).

4. Continue in this rhythm for 8-16 repetitions, and begin to lift your torso upward and decrease the lunges so that the body is more upright. Continue to alternate the arms swings and leg lifts. Keep the abdominals tight to support the back. Keep the back straight and the legs long. Slowly bring the legs closer to the ground. Eventually keep your feet on the ground and allow your arms to keep swinging with your torso gently twisting and then come to a rest. Finish with a deep breath and a full-arm circle overhead.

◆ Sun Worship ◆

abdominals, gluteals, quadriceps

1. Stand with your legs slightly apart, knees and toes facing forward. Soften the knees so you feel your hips have been lowered to the earth a bit and you feel more "planted" or stable. Place your hands in front of your abdominals with your palms facing your belly.

2. Push your hips out to the right, then circle them counterclockwise around front (as in a pelvic tilt) to the left side and continue the circle around to the back (pointing the tailbone backward so that you are arching your lower back) (*a* through *d*).

3. As you circle your hips, reach both arms in the same direction out to the right, then circle them along with your hips counterclockwise to the front away from the body, then to the left, then complete the circle back to the belly.

4. Begin with a deep inhalation before you start to move. As you start to circle your hips and arms, gently exhale. Begin to inhale halfway through the circle when the arms are out in front, and continue to inhale as you circle the hips and bring your arms back to center.

5. Repeat in the reverse direction (clockwise), beginning by pushing your hips left and circling clockwise around front toward the right side.

6. Imagine as you inhale that you are drawing the energy, the power of the sun, into your belly and gently exhaling your energy out as you breathe out. The sun's energy is a very healing power.

◆ Mother Nature Prayer ◆

body-mind-earth connection

1. After you have completed Sun Worship, allow yourself to stand in silence with your hands over your belly (*a*). Breathe deeply for several seconds or minutes, feeling the sensations of your body and listening to the sounds of nature. Feel your feet planted on the Earth. Feel the energy from the Earth rise up through you. Feel your body's energy reach down into the Earth. Close your eyes and sense this again. Allow yourself to make any meditative thought or affirmation you wish. After you feel relaxed and silent, gently open your eyes and allow the sights around you to come slowly back to you.

2. Look in all directions at all the nature that is around you. Gently reach your arms first low to the ground, then out to the front, and then up to the sky (*b*). Reach the whole body up to the sky with a deep inhale and gently exhale as you bring the arms and hands back to your belly, back to you. Hold. Then repeat as many times as you wish.

Tai Chi Workout

As you become comfortable with these exercises, practice performing them with fluidity, moving smoothly and gracefully from one exercise and movement to the next. The order of exercises here allows easy transition from one to the other. Think of this program as one complete segment or dance. The dance may be done very slowly for fluidity and stretch or more quickly with greater intensity for strength and power. Vary the rhythms for each exercise depending on your goal, mood, and energy level. You can modify these exercises any way you wish so that they feel comfortable.

An example of a tai chi segment might begin with Nature Worship. This will help focus your attention, bringing you into the present moment and connecting you with nature. Hold this position for a moment before beginning the following tai chi series or dance. You will notice this segment involves eight repetitions of each exercise sequence before moving on to the next. However, you may also try moving through one repetition of each of them to create a more interesting and complex sequence. Focus on moving through all the movements and from one exercise to the next as fluidly as possible. This will require great focus, balance, control, and strength.

1. Picking Up Grass—Perform eight times in the parallel position.
2. Picking Up Grass—Perform eight times in the turned out position.
3. Push/Pull (remember to turn your legs parallel)—Perform eight times.
4. Parting the Wild Horse's Mane—Perform the entire sequence eight times. (One sequence equals working on both the right and left sides.)
5. Reaping—Perform the entire sequence (right and left sides) eight times.
6. Flying—Perform the entire sequence eight times.
7. Soaring—Perform the entire sequence eight times.
8. Close with Sun Worship and Mother Nature Prayer.

5

Adding Power to Your Performance

Rugged walking is a rigorous activity requiring a good deal of strength. Muscular strength significantly influences the comfort, safety, and effectiveness of your rugged walk. Strength is important to both the physical and mental power of your performance. Being physically stronger helps you feel more confident in your abilities and therefore more confident in yourself. Take each step with muscle power and will power. Strength and anaerobic muscle training are essential components of a well-rounded health and fitness program. They enhance your physical capacity: strength, endurance, power, and overall performance. The rugged walker program takes your strength training outdoors, which can be much more motivational than training indoors. The inspirational power of nature will give a boost to your will power. It may even give you a whole new perspective on exercise.

This chapter first presents 22 strength-training resistance exercises. Some of these incorporate the use of a resistance band (such as Dynaband, a commercially available elastic resistance band), and others use the natural terrain to provide added resistance and variety. In the second part of the chapter, you'll learn 18 terrain drills that promote power, balance, agility, and strength. The final part of the chapter presents 11 arm drills to develop your arm muscles.

Strength Training

You exercise to look good and feel better, and strength training plays a more significant role in the process than you may have once thought. Strength training significantly improves posture and function, thereby enhancing physical performance. You may never end up playing a sport, but you forget that the normal tasks of everyday life can be just as demanding in many ways. Strength training not only increases your strength, but it also helps maintain muscle mass. As you age, you lose muscle and therefore become weaker. Strength training helps slow this process down. Muscle is also significant in the process of weight loss because it is the energy-consuming tissue of the body. The more conditioned muscle, the greater the muscle mass you have, the higher your metabolic rate, and therefore the greater your caloric expenditure. Strength training also prevents osteoporosis. Whenever you put stress on the bones, such as when you strength train, they respond by becoming stronger. Therefore, conditioning the muscular system also conditions the skeletal system.

Strength training can dramatically improve appearance. Without going on a diet, you can change the shape and look of your body. Cut inches off your waist, hips, and thighs by strength training. The body is composed of lean body mass—muscle, bones, and organs—and body fat. A body fat measurement gives you the percentage of your makeup that is lean body mass and the percentage that is fat. Your goal is to keep this measurement within healthy ranges. Strength training alone can improve your body composition. Without losing any weight, you can still lower your body fat percentage by increasing your muscle mass. In addition, your muscles are firmer, giving you a more fit and toned appearance. And if you combine the strength training with aerobic training, weight loss will be much more significant. Studies have found that people who trained with weights as well as exercised aerobically lost more weight and lost it faster than those who exercised only aerobically for longer periods of time, and the loss was more permanent.

Strength-Training Guidelines

A strength-training program is very easy to design; there is no need to go to the gym. It can be performed very effectively at home or on your rugged walk. The most important thing about training is that it be performed properly. If performed improperly, it may do more harm than good. You need to take the time to understand the proper form and technique of the exercise in order to prevent injury and ensure effectiveness. Some of the drills in this chapter involve impact or deep knee flexion, or both. So if you have any knee or back problems, choose other less dramatic movements for your drills.

Resistance or weight can be applied in exercise in a number of ways. It can be created manually by generating a certain amount of tension or resistance within the muscle (see the discussion of activated position in chapter 2) and using the weight of a body part. For example, when conditioning the abdominals, such as in abdominal curls, manual resistance is created by using the upper body, head, neck, and shoulders as the weight to be lifted manually by the abdominals. Lunging up a hill is another example of manual resistance. You are using the weight of your body to be lifted up the hill in order to strengthen your hips and thighs. For greater resistance, use external weights, such as dumbbells, weight machines, or resistance bands. In the rugged walker program, you can use rocks, logs, and different incline grades of the terrain.

When trying to decide how much weight to use, it is very important that, whatever you use, you are able to work your muscle through a full range of motion to ensure the safety and effectiveness of the exercise. Trying to lift too much weight will usually inhibit a full range of motion and thus will cause strain and improper movement, possibly resulting in injury. If the weight is too heavy and you are unable to work the muscle through the full range of motion, you will also compromise optimal conditioning of the muscle. Working with weights that are too heavy will also compromise your body alignment. As you attempt to lift a weight that is too heavy for the particular muscle that you are trying to condition, other muscle groups that are not intended to be involved in the exercise will probably become engaged. This may result in stress and strain on other areas of your body and may minimize the conditioning benefit to the intended muscle because it is being greatly assisted and thus not doing the work itself. I recommend choosing a weight to start with that will fatigue the muscle within two sets of eight repetitions of an exercise for that particular muscle.

When beginning a weight-training program, you should begin with low weight and gradually increase when you can easily handle this level of resistance. For example, a beginner may want to start a program with manual resistance exercises (without weights) combined with some band work (using an elastic resistance band such as the Dynaband) before working with weights. Some people prefer to continue to use only manual resistance exercises, which is certainly effective. However, keep in mind that the strength and conditioning gains will be less than those which may be achieved by using greater resistance, such as with weights or elastic bands. Strength is gained by working a muscle to the point of fatigue. During the training process, the muscle fibers tear down, only to be repaired more strongly during rest between workouts. The muscles are better able to resist more stress—that is, lift more weight—the next time.

The frequency of training has an effect on the rate and degree of strength gain. Infrequent training does little to support the training effect. It is recommended by the American College of Sports Medicine that strength training is best achieved by a program of a minimum of two sessions per week, performing 8 to 12 repetitions of each exercise. When you are able to perform these repetitions easily, increase the weight by approximately 5 to 10 percent each week. Your program should consist of 8 to 10 exercises addressing all the major groups of the body. It is important that you do not exercise the same muscle group within a 48-hour period as this may cause overuse and strain. Strength training will firm up muscle, and the training technique depends on the degree to which a person wants to "bulk up." A technique consisting of low weight with many repetitions will develop less strength and bulk but may emphasize muscle definition, whereas a program consisting of high weight with fewer repetitions will develop greater strength and bulk. Working with heavy weight usually emphasizes conditioning of the belly, or middle section, of the

◆ Nature provides the optimal weight-training studio—fresh air, beauty, and resistance.

muscle, and this results in the thickening or "bulking up" of the muscle. The exercises provided in this chapter are designed with the intention of improving strength, muscle definition, and good posture. I therefore recommend that you perform routines of lower rather than heavier weights and more repetitions.

When doing strength-training exercises, it is very important to practice proper posture, neutral spine/neutral mind, mind in the muscle, and activated position (see chapters 2 and 3). Paying attention to good body alignment and using these body-mind techniques will greatly enhance conditioning, ensuring safety and optimal effectiveness. Proper breathing technique is also important to the

Women and Weights

Many women have shied away from strength training because of the concern that they would "bulk up." The possibility of bulking up is determined by essentially two factors: genetics and the training technique. Generally, most women do not have the capacity to bulk up as men do. However, some women inherently do have more muscle than others, and their bodies are very responsive to strength training. The degree of bulk or muscle development can be controlled through the strength training technique. Do many repetitions with less weight if you don't want prominent muscles. Do fewer repetitions with more weight to develop prominent muscles.

effectiveness and safety of your strength training. It is recommended that you practice relaxed, deep breathing while you train. However, if your program is relatively intense, you may want to exhale on the part of the exercise that requires the greatest exertion, or during the concentric contraction, and inhale on the part of the exercise that is less exertional, or during the eccentric contraction. A concentric contraction is when we contract and shorten a muscle to lift (or move) a weight. The biceps, for example, contract and shorten to move your forearm to lift a weight up toward your shoulder. To lower the weight, the biceps remain contracted while they lengthen to lower your arm back down; this is an eccentric contraction.

Terrain Strength-Training Exercises

Rugged walking conditions the whole body because it engages both the upper and the lower body, unlike other aerobic activities such as stair climbing or cycling, which engage only the lower body. The arm pump, which is vital to the efficiency, speed, and power of the walk, as well as the arm drills condition the upper body: the arms, shoulders, chest, and back. The hip flexors, gluteals, quadriceps, and tibiales of the lower body are conditioned by rugged walking and the terrain drills. Rugged walking also conditions the abdominals because it requires a great deal of strength from them for stability and support while traversing the rugged terrain.

It is fun to integrate muscle-conditioning circuit training into your rugged walking workout. Or you may want to perform a series of muscle-conditioning exercises as a separate workout after your rugged walk or at another time. But if you do these exercises as a separate workout, it is important that you warm up first with low-level aerobic exercise and mild, rhythmic stretches. In circuit training you alternate a few minutes of moderate aerobic activity, such as walking, with a few minutes of muscle-conditioning exercises. You can add circuits by merely playing with the obstacles and "equipment" (rocks, logs, tree branches, stumps, hills) in your natural environment. A well-rounded program includes exercises for the different muscle groups of the whole body. For example, hike for five minutes, and then slow down to perform leg lunges for strength training of the hip and thigh. Hike again for five minutes, and then slow your pace to walking while performing military presses with rocks for strengthening of the shoulder and arm.

On the following pages you will find a variety of exercises designed for the rugged walker program to help you become stronger in your upper back, chest, shoulders, biceps, triceps, abdominals, and hip and thigh muscles. You will enjoy using the terrain in these exercises because it is great fun to condition your body using nature as your training ground. A detailed section devoted to abdominal training is included because this muscle group plays a very important role in your posture and therefore in all your movements.

The proper technique for the following exercises is presented so that you can exercise safely and effectively and so that you know how best to modify them to fit the terrain. Since you are out in the rugged world, you should pay attention to your footing so that you don't injure yourself. Also, pay attention to how much tension and stress you are putting on your knees and back when climbing on and off logs and rocks. If you have knee or back problems, you should use very low obstacles for stepping exercises or perform these exercises on the ground.

Although all the following strengthening exercises may be performed without weights (using manual resistance), many descriptions and photos illustrate the use of a resistance band. Using resistance bands is an easy and fun way to take your strength-training program for your upper body "on the road." With these portable products the top of a mountain or the beach can become your exercise studio. For some added fun—or if you don't have a resistance band—try other ways of adding resistance, such as rocks, logs, steps, or whatever else you find in your environment.

If you are using a resistance band such as the Dynaband, be sure not to wrap it around your hand too tightly. I usually recommend that you do not wrap it, but just hold it. Experiment with the band so that you get used to manipulating it to create different amounts of resistance. Remember, you should use a resistance that allows full range of motion. Resistance using the band is created by how far you stretch it. The greater the stretch, the greater the resistance. Before you begin each set of exercises, take a test repetition so that you can establish how much resistance you want to work with. Simply change the resistance, or stretch of the band, by moving your hands to different positions on the band. The closer together your hands are on the unstretched band, the stronger the stretch will be and therefore the greater the resistance. The farther apart your hands are on the band, the weaker the stretch and the lower the resistance. When you have stretched the band to the full range of motion of your muscle and feel the resistance of the stretch, be sure not to let the band pull you back quickly to your original position. The conditioning benefit comes not only from the resistance created by stretching the band, but also from resisting the band pulling you back quickly to the original position. Therefore, always return to the original position slowly and with control.

When you perform the upper-body exercises during circuit training in your rugged walker workout, remember to keep walking or marching in place so that your heart rate and breathing do not fall too far below your aerobic training zone. Then when you resume your aerobic training, your system will not have to work so hard to catch up to your desired level of intensity. Walking in place will ensure a safe and effective transition from your circuit training back to your aerobic exercise. The same is true when you perform lower-body exercises. In order to keep your intensity up while performing these exercises, make sure to use a large range of motion, steep grades, or quick-paced repetitions so that your heart rate does not drop too low.

◆ Chest Press ◆

pectorals

Hold your arms opened wide to the sides at shoulder height. Bend your elbows so that your hands are up toward the sky. Close your arms bringing your elbows together in front of your breastbone. Focus on leading inward with your elbows as you close the arms and concentrate on contracting the chest (pectoral) muscles rather than using your shoulder muscles to bring the arms in. Slowly return to the open position. Repeat two sets of eight repetitions.

◆ **Pull-Backs** ◆

upper back: rhomboids, trapezius

Hold your arms close together out in front of you at shoulder height. Keep a soft, relaxed bend in the elbows. Keeping your arms at shoulder height, open them out to the sides and slightly behind your body. Pull back leading with your elbows. Feel the stretch in your chest and the contraction in your upper back between your shoulder blades and behind your shoulders. Slowly return to the closed position. Repeat two sets of eight repetitions.

◆ Lat Pull-Downs ◆

mid- and lower back: latissimus dorsi

Hold your arms up over your head with your hands close together. Pull your elbows down at your sides toward your waist. As you pull down, draw the elbow very slightly behind your body. Feel the contraction in your back, along the sides of your back, and toward the mid- to lower back. Slowly return your arms to the overhead position. Repeat two sets of eight repetitions.

◆ **Bicep Curls** ◆

arm: biceps

Keep your elbows close to your waist and raise your hands (palm up) toward your shoulder. Create a 90-degree angle or smaller at your elbow joint. Slowly lower your arms to the beginning position. When using resistance, step on one end of the band with your left foot and hold the other end of the band in your right hand. Stretch the band by raising your right hand up toward your shoulder. Perform a set of repetitions with your palm turned up and then a set of repetitions with your palm turned down. Repeat two sets of eight repetitions. Repeat with the left arm.

♦ Lateral Raises ♦

shoulder: deltoid, rotator cuff

Begin with your arms down at your sides, and hold your elbows slightly bent. Raise your arms up and slightly higher than your shoulders. Keep the outside of your arms facing up to the sky and the inside of your arms facing the ground throughout the movement. Feel the contraction in the top of your shoulder. When using a resistance band, stand on the band with your right foot and hold the other end of the band in your left hand. Raise your left arm up to your shoulder. Lower slowly to the beginning position. Repeat two sets of eight repetitions. Repeat with the other arm.

For a variation, stretch the band by pulling your hand straight up to your chest, keeping your hand close to your body. As you are pulling up, raise your elbow slightly higher than your shoulder. Feel the contraction in the top of your shoulder.

◆ External Rotation ◆

shoulder: deltoid, rotator cuff

Begin with a lateral raise (see page 103). Hold it here as you rotate your arms outward and toward the back (so that your forearm rotates toward the sky and backward). Feel the contraction in the back of your shoulder joint. Rotate slowly back to the forward position. Repeat two sets of eight repetitions. Now repeat with the other arm.

◆ Triceps Press ◆

arm: triceps

Extend your right arm back behind you. Holding your arm in place, bend your elbow to bring your forearm and hand forward and toward your shoulder. Extend it back again. Support your torso with your left hand resting on your left thigh. Feel the contraction in the back of your arm very close to your shoulder. Repeat two sets of eight repetitions. Repeat with the left arm.

When using a resistance band, lunge forward with your left leg and put the end of the band under your left foot. Take the other end in your right hand. Hold the right arm back behind your right hip and slowly bend your right elbow so that your hand comes toward your right shoulder. This will relax the band a bit. Then straighten your arm. Feel the contraction in the back of your upper arm as you stretch the band. Return slowly to the bent-elbow position. Repeat two sets of eight repetitions. Repeat the exercise with the left arm.

◆ **Military Press** ◆

shoulders and arms: deltoids, triceps

Bend your elbows to raise your hands up in front of your shoulders and then push your arms up over head until your arms are straight. Be sure not to lock your elbows. Lower slowly and feel the contraction in your arms and shoulders. Repeat two sets of eight repetitions.

◆ Chin-Ups ◆

arms and back: biceps, latissimus dorsi

You know these. Find a branch that you can hang from. Place your hands, palms down, on the branch, and bend your knees to lift your feet off the ground. Slowly pull your body up so that your chin comes up over the branch. If it is too difficult to pull up your whole body, lower your feet and share some of your body weight with the ground. How much weight you allow to rest on your feet will determine how much weight you are lifting with your arms and therefore how intense your chin-up is. Repeat several times. Feel the contraction in your biceps and in your back. For variation, reverse your grip on the branch so that your palms are face up.

◆ Push-Backs ◆

chest and arms: pectorals, triceps

Stand about two feet (about 60 centimeters) or so from a wall and face it. Place your palms on the wall, fingers pointing up, and with your arms straight in front of you at shoulder height. Your hands are spaced a bit wider apart than your shoulders. Lean your weight into the wall by bending your elbows. Lower your chest until it is almost touching the wall. Then push back so that your arms are straight. Feel the contraction in your chest and in the back of your upper arms. Repeat several times. Variation: Stand closer and turn your back to the wall. Extend your arms behind you and place your palms on the wall. Lean your weight into your arms and bend your elbows to lean your body into the wall. Then straighten your arms. Repeat several times.

◆ **Push-Ups** ◆

chest and arms: pectorals, triceps

This exercise is similar to the push-back but is more advanced and requires more strength. Lie face down in the grass instead of against a wall. Place your hands in the grass just next to your shoulders. Your elbows are bent and pointed up to the sky. Keep your legs straight and your toes pointed to the ground. Push your body up out of the grass while keeping it as straight as possible. Compress your abdominals to prevent your lower back from arching. Then slowly lower your body back to the ground.

If this feels too difficult, move your hands a little farther out to the sides of your shoulders and bend your knees so that your feet come off the ground. Cross your ankles. When you push up, rest your body weight on your knees rather than on your toes. Feel the contraction in your chest and in the back of your upper arms. Repeat several times.

◆ **Straddle Walking** ◆

hips and thighs: quadriceps, gluteals, adductors

While straddling a log, feet on the ground, and your knees in a semisquat position, walk forward. Try one set with knees facing forward and another set with knees turned out. Walk until you feel fatigue in your thighs. Keep your hands on your hips. The lower you squat, the more intense the exercise.

◆ **Squat** ◆

hips and thighs: gluteals, quadriceps, adductors

Stand with your legs farther apart than your hips, knees and toes facing straight ahead. Keep your abdominals compressed for support as you bend your legs to lower your hips down as if you were going to sit. Be sure to keep your body weight back on your heels rather than on your toes; keep your heels on the ground and your knees up over your heels as much as possible (letting your knees lean out over your toes will put stress on the knee joint). Do not bend your knees more than 90 degrees. Stand back up and concentrate on contracting your buttocks. Repeat several times. Try performing the squat with your legs turned out. Contract your buttocks to keep your legs rotated out at the hip.

For more resistance stand on top of a step, log, or rock not much higher than a foot (30 centimeters) or so. Step one leg sideways off the log and squat. Leave the other leg on the log. Push from the squat back onto the top of the log. Squat off the log with the other leg. The higher the log or rock, the more intense the exercise. Be sure not to squat so low that you feel stress on the knee joints. Repeat 8 to 10 times, alternating legs. Rest and repeat again.

◆ Lunges ◆

hip, thigh: gluteals, quadriceps, hamstrings

Lunge forward on your right leg so that your right knee is at a 90-degree angle. Keep your knee over your heel rather than over your toes. Allow your left heel to come off the ground and your left knee to bend as you lunge. Feel the contraction in your right quadriceps. Come up out of the lunge and return your right leg to your left leg. Next lunge on your left leg. Repeat eight times.

Try these variations on the lunge:

1. Lunge on your right leg. Keep your left leg straight in back, but allow the heel to come off the ground. Come up out of the lunge, then lunge into your left leg.

2. Keep your left leg straight and lunge forward on your right leg. As you come up out of the lunge raise your left leg up in the back before bringing it forward for the next lunge. Feel the contraction in your left hamstring and buttocks.

3. Lunge uphill or on stairs.

4. For more resistance, stand facing a log or rock. Lunge your right leg up onto the top of the log. Be sure that your right knee is not leaning out over your toes as you lunge. Push off with the right leg and bring it together with the left leg on the ground. Feel the contraction in your thighs and buttocks. Repeat 8 to 10 times, either all on one side then the other, or alternating legs. Rest and repeat.

◆ Calf Raises ◆

calves

Stand on the edge of a curb or rock on the balls of your feet with one heel hanging off the edge. Rise up on the balls of your feet and then lower back down. To make it more difficult, lower your heels below the edge of the curb and then raise them up. Feel the contraction in your calves. Repeat raising and lowering for two sets of eight repetitions.

◆ Step Strength Training ◆

hips and legs: quadriceps, gluteals, calves

Find a log, rock, or curb that is about 10 inches (25 centimeters) or so high. Keep in mind that the higher the step, the more intense the exercise and the more pressure on the knee. Facing the log, try performing each of the following stepping patterns for a set of eight repetitions. Each exercise has its own distinct stepping pattern.

1. Leading with the same leg. Step up with the right, then up with the left; step down with the right, then down with the left. This pattern is up right, up left, down right, down left; then up right, up left, down right, down left. Repeat, leading with the left leg.

2. Alternating leading legs. Step up with the right, then up with the left, step down with the right, then just tap the left down on the ground and step up with it to begin the pattern on the other side. This pattern is up right, up left, down right, tap down left; then up left, up right, down left, tap down right.

3. Step up on your right foot, then lift your left knee. This pattern will naturally alternate leading legs. The pattern is up right, lift left knee, down left, down right; up left, lift right knee, down right, down left.

4. Step up on your right foot, then lift the left leg to the back. This series has the same pattern as variation 3, but instead of lifting the knee to the front, raise the leg to the back.

5. Face sideways to the curb and step up on your right foot, then lift the left leg out to the side. Repeat 8 to 12 times, then turn around to use the other leg.

♦ Back Extensions ♦

low back: erector spinae

Lying on your stomach, lengthen your body by stretching through the length of your spine. Keep your face down. Slowly lift your head and chest slightly off the ground. Keep your legs down and contract your buttocks to provide support to your lower back. Lower slowly to the beginning position. Repeat several times.

 Adding Your Own Exercises

There are many, many more terrain strength-training exercises that you can create. Just look around you and see what you can climb on, hang from, push against, step over, jump across, and so on. You get the idea. Combine arm exercises with leg exercises to make them more challenging and effective for full-body conditioning. For example, combine lat pull-downs with squats, lateral raises with lunges, or biceps curls with calf raises. Refer to page 000 for additional descriptions of arm drills that can be combined with these strength-training exercises.

Abdominal Exercises

Rugged walking is a terrific way to condition the abdominal muscles (commonly called the abs). The abs come into play in absolutely everything you do. The abdominal wall is the base of your resistance and power. It is the primary muscle group involved in proper body alignment because it supports the natural curves of the spine. The abs significantly affect your performance: the safety and efficiency of your body mechanics and your body's ability to absorb shock. Therefore, the abs are the focus muscle group in good posture and proper back care.

The abdominal wall is also the center of your being. Breathing deeply into the abdominal area or belly brings your mind more in tune and in focus with the sensations of your body. Through breathing practice, you train yourself to be more aware of the experience of the present moment. When you become aware of your poor posture and aching back, for example, you usually adjust yourself by compressing and lifting up on your abs and lengthening through your spine to stand taller.

To condition the abs properly, you need to understand a bit about their construction and function: their anatomy and kinesiology. An awareness of exactly where the muscles are located and how they are oriented (which direction the fibers run) will help you know how to move or exercise the muscle efficiently and effectively. In order to condition the abs most effectively, you need exercises that work the abdominals in all the different directions of movement that they can accommodate: twisting, forward flexion, and compression. Simply performing forward flexions will not very effectively condition the muscle fibers that run in a diagonal direction. Performing forward flexions in a diagonal direction or with a twist will be much more effective. Forward flexions are not as effective in conditioning the transverse group, the muscle fibers that run horizontally, as compressions are.

Most of the exercises are performed in the supine position (lying on your back) in order to protect the back and to be able to most effectively apply the resistance of gravity. For proper positioning, lie on the floor with your knees bent and the soles of your feet flat on the floor. Keep your feet and knees in line with your hips. Your toes should be facing straight ahead or just slightly turned in. When appropriate to the exercise, your head and neck

Abdominal Anatomy

Location: Front middle torso from the ribs to the pubic bone

Function: Flexion, rotation, and stabilization of the torso

Orientation: There are basically four layers of muscle that form the abdominal wall. The external obliques form the outer layer of the lateral abdominal wall. The fibers run diagonally across the midsection of your torso from the edges of your lower ribs down to your pelvic/hip bones. Deeper and running in the opposite diagonal to the external obliques from your pelvic/hip bones up to your lower ribs and to the rectus are your internal obliques. Together these muscles are primarily responsible for diagonal forward flexion and twisting. The rectus is in the center of your abdominal region and has fibers that run vertical from your sternum to your pubis bone. It is most responsible for forward

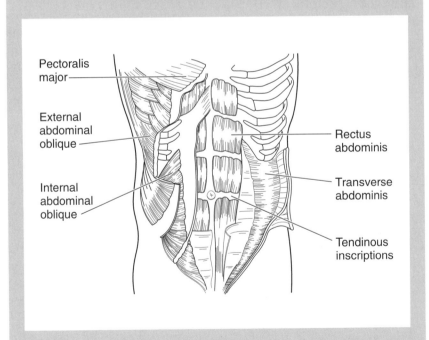

Continued on next page

Abdominal Anatomy—continued

flexion. The tranversalis muscle lies deepest and its fibers run horizontally. This muscle is primarily responsible for twisting and compression of the abdomen. All four muscles work intimately together to perform the many movements of your torso and form a very intricate and unique net of support to your spine.

should be supported in the hands or an arm cradle. You can create different levels of resistance with your arm placement. There will be less weight or resistance for your abs to lift if you cross your arms over your chest than if you have them held behind your head. If you are just beginning, you may want to start your abdominal conditioning program with compressions.

When performing any of the following exercises, these guidelines will be helpful.

1. Maintain *activated position* throughout the exercise: abdominals are compressed (isometric contraction) throughout the full range of motion and not released between repetitions. Focus on *mind in the muscle* and work the eccentric contraction as much as the concentric contraction. Maintain neutral spine, or the normal lumbar arch.

2. Breathe comfortably and in your own rhythm; it is often recommended that you exhale on the curl, or the concentric contraction, and inhale on the opening, or eccentric contraction.

3. You may want to vary the tempo of your movement to provide a different sensation in your conditioning. However, be sure that your range of motion is appropriate for the tempo. For example, holding your torso in a curled position and performing small little crunches in this position will accommodate a fast tempo. But full-range-of-motion abdominal curls will be less effective if the tempo is too fast.

◆ Compressions ◆

all abdominals, especially transverse abdominals

Lie on your back. Place your hands, palms down, on the ground at your sides. To perform a compression, sense your abdominal wall and pull your abdominal muscles in. Focus on compressing the entire abdominal wall toward the spine. The compression begins at the edges of the ribs, hipbones, and the sides of the torso and moves in toward the center of the abdominal area. Imagine the spokes of a wheel being compressed by pushing in at the hub of the wheel. The ribs should feel pulled in toward the spine and down toward the naval. It is important not to compress the abs so much that you flatten out the lower lumbar curve of your back, but rather to support it—not allowing it to exaggerate its arch. Also, you do not want to compress the abs so much that you feel you cannot breathe. Remember, breathing happens by expanding your diaphragm. Practice breathing deeply using the diaphragm as you hold this compression. You will have the sense of wanting to expand the chest and belly when breathing in. However, remember that the diaphragm expands down toward the hips to provide increased lung capacity. Practice compressing and releasing the abdominal wall in sets of eight repetitions.

◆ Forward and Diagonal Curls ◆

obliques and rectus abdominis

Cradle your head and neck by placing your arms behind your neck and letting your head rest in them. Compress the abdominal wall—activated position—then slowly lift the shoulders up, curling the torso and bringing the ribs and sternum toward the hipbones. This is a forward curl that emphasizes the rectus abdominis. The activated position will help keep the abdominal wall compressed and flat: pressing in toward the spine during the curl rather than pushing out at the height of the curl (pushing out is common when performing abdominal curls, so be aware of how

you are doing). In the diagonal curl, one shoulder rises toward the opposite hip and thus is lifted slightly higher than the other shoulder. Diagonal curls emphasize the obliques. When uncurling, lower the shoulders toward the ground; however, be certain not to lay your shoulders back down completely onto the ground. This will cause you to release the tension, or activated position, in the abdominal wall. Keep your shoulders about half an inch (one centimeter) off the ground throughout the entire exercise. Perform the curls in sets of eight—eight forward curls, eight right diagonal curls, eight left diagonal curls—until you feel fatigue in the abs.

◆ Pelvic Tilts ◆

pelvic abdominal area

Place your hands, palms down, by your sides. Tilt your hips under by lifting your tailbone off the ground as you compress the abdominal wall. Pull or curl your tailbone and hipbones toward the ribs and sternum. This movement will flatten your lower back. Perform this slowly, focusing on the contraction in the pelvic region of your abdominals. Perform pelvic tilts in sets of eight until you feel fatigue.

◆ Reverse Curls ◆

abdominal wall with emphasis on rectus abdominis

This is essentially the same exercise as the pelvic tilt but with the added resistance or weight of your legs. Place your hands, palms down, on the ground at your sides. Lift both legs and cross them at the ankles. Allow the knees to bend and your thighs to drop toward the torso (feel the weight of the legs press down toward your body). They are your added weight or resistance. Curl your pelvis by lifting your tailbone off the ground and curling it toward your sternum. Try not to use your legs for assistance: don't pull them toward your chest as you lift your tailbone. Keep your legs stationary; they are merely weights and are not involved in the action of the exercise. You may want to support your thighs in your hands so they are unable to provide momentum to the curl.

◆ Bent-Leg Lifts ◆

abdominal wall with emphasis on transverse muscles

This is a relatively advanced exercise and should be performed carefully. If at anytime you feel strain in your back, you should refrain from performing it until you feel stronger. Place your hands under your lower back so that your palms are on the ground and your fingers are spread out under your lower back, fingertips touching each other. Compress the abdominal wall so that you feel your back press against your fingers. It is important to keep the abdominals compressed enough throughout the exercise that the pressure on your fingers does not change.

The action in this exercise is to lift one or both legs (both legs is more difficult) very slowly off the ground while maintaining your back's pressure on your fingers. The legs should remain in the original bent-knee position, and the movement occurs only at the hip joint. The knee joint does not move. Then slowly lower your leg or legs to the ground. Repeat eight times. If you are working with one leg at a time, repeat eight times with one leg then eight times with the other leg. If the pressure on your fingers lessens while you are lifting your legs, your abdominals may not be strong enough for this exercise. If you are lifting both legs, try only one at a time.

 ## Abdominal Exercise Contraindications

It is important to be aware of exercise contraindications so that you do not hurt yourself and so that you condition effectively. Contraindications are positions or movements of the body that may predispose it to injury.

It is important to note that in most individuals, the power and the strength of the iliopsoas muscle group is usually stronger than the abdominals. And this imbalance between the abdominals and the iliopsoas muscle groups may cause lower back discomfort. The iliopsoas muscles (hip flexors) originate deep at the lower spine and cross the hip joint to attach at the inner side of the top of the femur (thighbone) to a protuberance called the lesser trochanter. They are responsible for flexing the leg at the hip as well as rotating it inward. This muscle group is very much involved in the mobility of your leg and therefore becomes very strong and conditioned from just normal daily activity.

When you perform an abdominal exercise involving the hip flexors (for example; sit-ups and leg raises to the front), these hip flexors will usually overpower the abdominals and perform most of the work. Since they are connected to the lower vertebrae of your back, they will pull these forward and cause stressful arching of the lower back. Some individuals' abdominals may be strong enough to override the arching of the back and keep it relatively stable. But most of us strain to hold the back from arching, and the abdominals end up pushing out somewhat from the strain. In this position usually only the rectus abdominis becomes really conditioned, and often so that it protrudes rather than lays flat, as we would like. It is very difficult to maintain the compression or flatness of the activated position in these types of exercises, and they therefore may do more harm than good.

Here is a list of things you should be careful *not* to do.

1. Do not pull on your head or neck while performing curls. This may strain your neck.

2. Do not overemphasize a flat back while performing curls. This is an ineffective position for optimal conditioning of the abs.

3. Do not perform arm exercises while doing abdominal work. These may distort your body alignment and distract your attention from effective conditioning of the abs.

4. Do not do full sit-ups, flat-leg curls (performing curls while your legs are straight), or straight-leg lifts. These exercises are contraindicated because they engage the hip flexor (iliopsoas) muscle group, which will aggravate the lower back.

Terrain Drills

Rugged walkers walk in all kinds of weather and on all kinds of terrain. The terrain around you provides a wonderful obstacle course in the most beautiful exercise studio in the world: the great outdoors. Terrain drills used in interval-training technique make rugged walking an intense challenge and much more fun than just simply walking. As you venture to the great outdoors to play over the rugged terrain, it will be fun to have some terrain training techniques. There are 18 terrain drills presented here, which are designed to promote power, strength, balance, and agility. They need not be difficult to be very effective. In fact, it is important that they be simple, easy, and comfortable so that you can perform them safely and concentrate more on your intensity, power, and effectiveness than on the complexity of movement.

It is important for effectiveness and injury prevention to understand the technique of the rugged walker terrain drills and to practice proper body alignment as you perform them. Drills that involve jumping should be done on flat, clear terrain. Remember to be aware of your footing at all times, so that you do not have an accident. Your most favorite drills will be ones that are most fun for you. Practice them often. You will have great fun designing your own drills by being spontaneous and playful with the terrain. Be sure to experiment with different terrains.

Many of the rugged walker drills resemble sport or dance movements. Performing these drills with speed will enhance anaerobic training. Performing them more slowly and with greater range of motion will use more muscle power (manual contraction) and therefore enhance muscular conditioning. Using more *muscle power* (mind in the muscle and activated position) than momentum will increase the intensity of work. Also, remember to use your arms in the drills for enhanced body alignment and a more effective full-body workout. Use the arm pump whenever there is no other arm movement specified or when you are speed walking.

Following are descriptions of how to perform each drill. Each drill works primary muscle groups, which are listed after the name of the drill. The drills can be used on various types of terrain: uphill, downhill, flat road, dirt path, over rocks and streams, in the sand, on the street, and so on. Different terrain will affect the intensity of the exercise. For example, speed walking in sand will be much more intense than on pavement. For safety and effectiveness, however, be certain to watch your footing and body alignment.

◆ Speed Walking ◆
full-body conditioning

Speed can be used on all types of terrain. Using proper walking and speed technique (see chapter 3), walk as fast as you can. Recover by walking at a more moderate pace for twice as long. Repeat several times.

◆ Groucho Walk ◆

quadriceps, gluteals, deltoids

Start walking, then bend your knees so you are in a deep lunge position. Make sure your knees stay over your heels (forming a 90-degree or wider angle at the knee) as you step forward. Walk quickly in this squat position while pumping your arms.

◆ Groucho Lay-Ups ◆

quadriceps, gluteals, deltoids, triceps

Take three Groucho steps beginning with your right foot, then hop on the third step (on your right foot), bringing your left knee up and landing on your right foot again. When you land, be sure to bend your knees to help absorb the impact. Take three Groucho steps beginning with your left foot, hop on your third step (on your left foot). Pump the arms as you Groucho walk and then swing them wider or shoot them overhead, as in basketball, when you hop. Continue to step-step-step-shoot (on the count of 1, 2, 3, 4).

◆ Lay-Up Series ◆

quadriceps, gluteals, deltoids, triceps

Alternate the hop and knee lift (lay-up move) on every step, like skipping. To make it more intense, remember the deeper the landing, the higher the jump. Swing your arms at your sides on the Groucho steps, and hold them at shoulder height on each hop. The arm opposite the lifted knee is in front and the other arm is out to the side.

◆ Hill Lunging ◆

quadriceps, gluteals, hamstrings, calves, deltoids

Take a long lunging step forward up a hill with your right leg, landing with your right knee bent (keeping the knee over the heel rather than forward over your toes) and your left leg straight in the back. Then, lifting out of your right knee and pushing off your left leg, swing the left leg through and lunge it forward. Continue to alternate the lead leg, swinging your arms up to shoulder height in opposition to your legs.

◆ Backward Groucho Walking Uphill ◆

hamstrings, gluteals, quadriceps

Be sure the way is clear of debris. Crouch low into the knees (however, avoid bending too low and putting stress on the knee) and Groucho walk up the hill backward. If you are on a flat surface, work to extend the leg backward as much as possible on each step. Emphasize working the gluteals.

◆ Hurdle Jumping ◆

quadriceps, gluteals, calves, deltoids

Take three Groucho steps and then a low, long leap on the fourth step (as if you were jumping a hurdle). Each time you leap forward, be sure to push strongly off the back leg and stay low to the ground. Swing your arms wide and in opposition to your legs. Repeat sequence (1, 2, 3, 4), leading with the other leg. If you use a 1-2-3 count (leaping on 3 rather than on 4), you will automatically alternate legs. It is fun to experiment with both rhythms.

◆ Gully Jumping ◆

gluteals, calves, deltoids

This exercise is similar to a football tire drill. Get into a semisquat position with your knees and toes facing forward, feet a little wider than hip's distance apart. Keeping your body low to the ground, push forward to leap from one leg to the other as you straddle the gully. Swing your arms wide and in opposition to your legs.

◆ Puddle Jumping ◆

quadriceps, gluteals

Find a puddle. Jump over it. Better yet, if you see a series of puddles, leapfrog over them. For safety and effectiveness, be sure to land on soft, relaxed knees. For more intensity, remember that the deeper you land, the higher you jump. However, be sure not to land too deeply and stress the knees.

◆ Jumping Jacks ◆

quadriceps, gluteals, hip adductors, calves, deltoids, trapezius

You know these. Stand with your legs together and arms down at your sides. Jump up and land with your legs apart. Keep your knees and toes facing straight ahead. Raise your arms out to your sides as you jump and up over your head as you land. As you land, bend your knees to absorb the impact and prepare for your next jump. Jump again, and land with your legs together. Bring your arms back down to your sides.

◆ Jack Squats ◆

quadriceps, gluteals, hip adductors, deltoids, trapezius

This drill uses the same movement as a jumping jack, but without the jump and with an emphasis on a deep squat. With knees and feet facing straight ahead, lift one leg out wide to the side and land in a deep squat position. As you come up out of the squat bring the other leg in and land in a semisquat with your legs together. Repeat, this time leading with the other leg. Use the arms as you would in a jumping jack.

◆ Squat Series ◆

quadriceps, gluteals, deltoids

Turn sideways to the direction you will be traveling. Step the lead leg out and squat low; bend the knees deeply (but no more than 90 degrees) so that your hips approach the level of your knees as closely as possible. Step the following leg in as you stand up. Raise the arms to shoulder height out to the sides as you squat and return them down to your sides when you stand up. You may want to perform a series of eight squats on the one side and then change lead legs. As you bring in the following leg, turn so that this leg is now leading in the direction you are going into the next squat. For more of a challenge alternate legs by rotating around on each step.

◆ Jalking ◆

full-body conditioning

Jalking—jog walking—is a fun speed technique you may want to try. It is a combination of walking and jogging that allows speed while keeping structural stress to a minimum. In essence, it is like jogging, except you work to keep your feet as close as possible to the ground by keeping your legs relatively straight. Allowing your feet to become airborne enhances your ability to go faster when speed walking. Incorporating the arm pump will really add power for a very high-intensity drill. You may feel silly doing this drill, but it is truly a great workout. So find a secluded spot and go for it!

◆ Jalk/Walk ◆

full-body conditioning

Alternate walking and jalking. Zigzag across a mountain road, on the beach, or in the street.

◆ Stair Climbing ◆

quadriceps, gluteals, calves

You can do many of these drills on the stairs in order to add greater intensity. Speed walk up the stairs. Take the stairs two or three at a time. Do this in a straddle position. Groucho walk up the stairs. Walk up backward. Lunge up the stairs three or four at a time. Jog up the stairs. Whichever drill you choose, be sure to pay particular attention to your footing so that you do not fall.

◆ Hill Jogging ◆

calves

On a steep hill, lean your body slightly forward (lean the whole body from your ankles) and jog up the hill. Jog more on the balls of your feet than on the full foot. Jog as quickly or as slowly as feels comfortable.

◆ Sprinting Downhill ◆

quadriceps

Just take off. Be certain, however, to control the run by using your abdominals for support to your back, using your hips and thighs to keep the strides small, and keeping your weight back in your heels. And for shock absorption, keep your knees soft. For safety, be sure to watch where you are stepping.

◆ Beach Drills ◆

calves, quadriceps, gluteals

Jogging or speed walking in the sand is a great low-impact aerobic exercise: Dodge the waves, jump over seaweed on the beach, hurdle over logs, walk along logs, climb up over rocks. All the other drills are fun in the sand too.

Balance and Agility Moves

Balance and agility are important for ease and safety of movement and maintaining good posture. It is fun to improve balance and agility by practicing movements that resemble dance steps or sport moves and by merely climbing up and over things. Experiment with your balance, for example, by walking on narrow beams, such as logs and curbs, and by standing on one foot on top of a rock while raising the other leg out to the side. Work with your agility by leaping over logs and gullies; climbing trees, rocks, and ridges; power-leaping over rough terrain; jumping on and off rocks; or running and doing a series of turns on the beach. Be creative and allow yourself to do sport and dance type moves to help develop your sense of balance and improve your agility.

Arm Drills

These arm drills are fun to do during your moderate or recovery walking intervals. They will promote strength and definition of your upper body and keep your workout more challenging and motivating. The tempo of these exercises should be half the tempo of the pace of your walk. It is important to mention that by focusing a good deal of attention on mind in the muscle and especially activated position, the intensity and therefore the effectiveness of these exercises will be far greater. Perform as many repetitions as it takes until you feel fatigue in the particular muscle group you are working. Adding low weights, such as rocks, will increase the intensity of the muscle work. For variation, both arms may be worked together or in an alternating pattern.

◆ Backward Swing ◆
rear deltoid, triceps

Keeping your elbows straight, push your arms backward so that you feel a stretch in front of your shoulder and a contraction in the back. Let your arms swing forward, and then push them back again.

◆ Triceps Kickbacks ◆
triceps, rear deltoids

Hold your arms straight and raised behind you. Bend the elbows, bringing the lower arms in, and then press them back out, straightening the elbows. Push out with your palms facing back. Feel the contraction up the back of the upper arm.

◆ Lateral Raises ◆

deltoids, trapezius

With your arms down, bend your elbows 90 degrees. Raise your arms out to the sides slightly above your shoulders. Feel the contraction at the top of your shoulders. For more resistance, keep your arms straight through the exercise.

◆ Anterior Raises ◆

deltoids

Raise your arms out front slightly higher than your shoulders. Keep your arms straight and your palms facing the ground. Feel the contraction in the front of your shoulder. For a variation, hold your palms up.

◆ Chest/Back Press ◆

pectorals, upper back, deltoids

Raise your arms out to the sides to shoulder height, palms forward. Bend your elbows 90 degrees so your hands are reaching up to the sky. Bring your elbows together in front of your chest. Focus on your chest muscles, and contract them strongly as you bring the arms in. Then open your arms as far back as possible, feeling the muscles in your upper back contract.

◆ Military Press ◆

deltoids, triceps

Raise your hands to your shoulders bending your elbows up and out to the side. Press both your arms straight up over your head. Feel the contraction over the top of your shoulder.

♦ Bicep Curls ♦

biceps

Keep your upper arms against the sides of your body. Bend the arms at the elbow, bringing your hands, palms up, toward your shoulders. Feel the contraction in the front of your upper arm. For variation, keep your palms facing down.

♦ Raised Biceps Curls ♦

biceps, deltoids

Hold your arms out in front of you at shoulder height, palms up. Bend your elbows, bringing your hands in toward your shoulders. Feel the contraction in the front of the shoulder and on top of your upper arm.

♦ Rotator Cuff Drill ♦

shoulder rotators, chest, and upper back

Hold your arms straight down at your sides. Rotate your arms inward as far as you can and then rotate them outward as far as you can. Feel your chest, shoulder, and upper back contract to perform the rotation. Variation: Hold your arms out to your sides at shoulder height, palms down, and bend your elbows to a 90-degree angle. Your forearm and hand are parallel with the ground. Rotate your arms from the shoulder as far back as possible and then rotate them forward as far as possible.

◆ Push/Pull ◆

pectorals, triceps, upper back

Hold your hands up at your chest (in front and close to your body). Push forward until your arms are straight. Then pull your hands back to your chest while bending your elbows. Pull your elbows as far behind your body as possible. Feel the contraction in your chest and the back of your upper arms when you push out and then in your biceps and upper back when you pull back.

◆ Upright Row ◆

deltoids

With your hands down at your sides, arms straight, bend your elbows and raise your hands up to your shoulder. Raise your elbows a little higher than your shoulder. Feel the contraction in the top of your shoulder.

Creating Your Own Activities

The drills and exercises in this chapter are only the beginning—much of the fun of the program is in creating your own drills. Allow yourself to be open to how your body feels, and let the terrain inspire you to move. If you want to condition for a particular sport, try to mimic that sports movement using the terrain. For example, if you were a skier you could jump downhill in a zigzag pattern just like you were slaloming down the mountain. To condition individual body parts, figure out a way to mimic the movement based on how your muscles move—like the lat pull-down shown earlier in the chapter.

There's no limit to what you can do. Be creative and let your imagination go! Don't worry, you can't come up with a drill or exercise that's "wrong", but be sure to do them safely.

CHAPTER

6

Rugged Walking Programs

Rugged walking means venturing off-road, off the beaten track. It means venturing into new realms to experience something new about yourself. Rugged walking is a personal challenge to use your whole self—body and mind—and to go beyond your current fitness level and your current perspective to open up to new and unlimited possibilities. The body will increase its physical fitness through playing in nature, the mind its mental capacity through acquiring new knowledge, and the spirit its expression through going on an adventure. Rugged walking requires not only muscle power, but great will power—power of spirit—too. So does life. Nature's terrain teaches you much about the terrain of life. Sometimes in life you want intensity to get you through the challenges as you hike over the rough terrain to reach new heights. And at times you want to go slower so that you can relax and contemplate the beauty around you: smell the trees, feel the breeze, and take in the views. Let nature's obstacles dictate your course. If you can climb it, climb it. If you can jump it, jump it. And if you must go around it, do it with power and patience.

This chapter presents rugged walker workouts for different fitness levels that will help you get started and stick to a rugged walking program. The idea is for you to use this information to create your own program. The rugged walker programs may be easily modified to accommodate your fitness level and personal goals, or simply pick out parts of the workouts and add them to your own ideas for your own personalized program. Keep in mind that the focus of this program is to be as creative as possible in using the natural environment to make your workout challenging, well-rounded, inspirational, and fun. You may want to use rugged walking as your main exercise program, or you may want to integrate it into your fitness regime as a cross-training activity. It is ideal for either purpose.

The Mountain Within

Who am I?
I am at the bottom
looking up.

The sky is gray.
Fog all around.

Cannot see the top.
I know it is there.

Would that I trust
God is there
the same way.
I slip.
It is rugged.

I know I can find
the right footing.
I keep trying.

Stay flexible
yet true.

At times,
it is very steep.

I fall.
It is rugged.

I ache with exhaustion.
Cannot go on.

I feel weak, inadequate.

I am not strong enough
to go through this.

I am not good enough.

I feel old.
It is rugged.

Then it eases
as the path levels out.
The mountain is forgiving.
Just when I need it most.

I push forward
no matter what.

I feel strong, liberated,
able to make the climb.

I see all
that is with me now.
The beauty is inspiring.

I trust
my every step.
The ground
beneath my feet.

I feel young and worthy.
I keep going,
ascending to a higher plane.

I am at the bottom
looking within.
I am a child of the Universe.

I am.

Anatomy of a Rugged Walking Workout

As with all exercise sessions, you begin with a warm-up in order to loosen up—elevate your heart rate and blood flow, activate the muscle groups, and prepare joints for the expected range of motion of the exercise—and to focus in—bring your awareness and attention to your body. You then increase the intensity to your aerobic training zone for a certain length of time, usually a minimum of 15 to 20 minutes. You may also want to add interval training for more intensity. Following or integrated into the aerobic training, you may want to perform some muscle-conditioning exercise circuits. You then cool down from the training zone to return your body's systems close to resting levels and to release the muscle tension that has built up as a result of exercise. Then finish the workout with stretching exercises for flexibility conditioning and with a few moments of meditation to enhance your body-mind connection and instill a sense of relaxation and well-being.

The Warm-Up

After completing a five- to seven-minute relaxed, brisk walk, slow your pace while making your stride and arm swings as long as possible. Then reach your arms overhead as you inhale, and lower them slowly to your sides as you exhale. Focus on releasing tension—physical and mental—as you exhale. As you prepare the body for exercise, you also should prepare the mind for the workout by bringing your attention—mind in the muscle—to the experience of the workout; don't allow yourself to be distracted by thoughts of other things. As you perform the stretching portion of the warm-up, bring your focus and concentration to your breath, to your body, to the present moment, and to the nature around you.

Continuing the warm-up, perform stretches that are slow and rhythmic and that emphasize large ranges of motion, for example, slow arm circles, shoulder rolls, shallow side-to-side lunges, arm reaches overhead, low back stretches, hip circles, and pelvic tilts. Begin stretching your neck and work downward through the shoulders. Gradually move on to the sides of the torso; chest; back (upper and lower); hip flexors and quadriceps; hamstrings, gluteals, and adductors; calves and tibiales; and the foot and ankle. Avoid static stretching (stretches held for 30 to 40 seconds) in your warm-up, as these are more conducive to flexibility conditioning than optimal warm-up. It is best to keep moving rhythmically through the stretches. The tai chi exercise Nature Worship (presented in chapter 4) is an excellent body-mind, rhythmic stretch for warm-up. After warming up, resume walking and focus on proper body alignment and stride techniques, as presented in chapter 3.

Aerobic Conditioning

Gradually pick up the pace until you feel you are in your aerobic training zone; you will feel warm, perhaps beginning to break a sweat, and your heart rate and breathing will increase. Soon you will feel yourself in what we call the *steady state:* this is when your level of exercise intensity plateaus and you feel that you are exercising steadily with "somewhat hard" exertion (13-14 on the Borg scale) and feel relatively comfortable. This steady-state training is an excellent time to focus on body-mind concepts: mind in the muscle, activated position (chapter 2), and proper walking techniques (chapter 3). The beginner rugged walker program focuses on steady-state aerobic training and proper walking techniques. As your aerobic fitness advances, you may want to add speed and terrain drill interval training, as presented in the intermediate and advanced programs.

Interval Training

After ten to fifteen minutes of fast-paced, steady-state walking, when you feel you are ready to work harder, begin your interval training. It is best to begin with one or two speed intervals, focusing on proper speed-walking techniques (chapter 3: arm pump and stride techniques). Then add intervals of terrain drills.

Each interval should include a recovery period at least twice as long as the high-intensity period: a ratio of 2 to 1. For example, one minute of speed walking should be followed with two minutes of moderate-intensity or steady-state walking. Or a distance of one block of sprinting uphill should be followed by two blocks of slow, shallow lunging uphill. For drills you find extremely intense, it is advisable to extend the recovery period. Get to know your body by tuning in and monitoring your response to exercise: focus on how hard you are breathing, how warm you feel, how tired your muscles are, and you will feel when your recovery period is enough. During the recovery interval you want to feel your body's response (heart rate, blood pressure, and breathing) decrease to moderate- or steady-state intensity. Refer to chapter 2, "Monitoring Your Exercise Intensity," for details. As you become more fit, you may want to try more advanced drills, lengthen the duration of the intense intervals, or add more intervals.

After you have practiced your interval segment and have allowed your body to return to a more moderate level of exertion, you may want to practice muscle-conditioning circuits or balance and agility drills. Balance and agility drills include such things as walking along a log, walking across rocks in a stream, climbing up trees and over fences, straddle-jumping puddles, balancing on stumps, and so on (see "Balance and Agility Moves" in chapter 5). These drills enhance your balance and agility and, most especially, are fun. This is an opportunity to tap into your creative adventurous spirit: the center of childlike energy so important to our vitality and enjoyment of life.

Muscle-Conditioning Circuits

Muscle-conditioning circuits, using the terrain strength-training exercises presented in chapter 5 as well as others you create, are integrated into the intermediate and advanced rugged walker programs. These circuits can be interspersed throughout the interval training or worked in as a separate segment after the interval-training segment. Before performing these exercises, take two minutes or so of lower-intensity walking to bring your heart rate into a more aerobic (rather than anaerobic) range. While performing these exercises, keep the legs moving rhythmically if you are not using them in the exercise to keep your heart rate from dropping too low, as advised in chapter 5. Marching in place or performing shallow squats or lunges is an excellent way to keep the legs involved while performing upper-body exercises. For example, gradually slow down from an intense terrain drill interval by changing to a brisk walk and then to marching in place. Keep marching while you prepare to use a resistance band and then perform a set of lat pulldowns. Return to a brisk walk and gradually pick up the tempo to

◆ Lunging uphill is a fun, high-intensity drill that is also ideal for conditioning hips and thighs.

your aerobic, or steady-state, walking pace, then gradually pick up the intensity in preparation for the next terrain drill or keep the pace moderate in preparation for the next muscle-conditioning circuit. Pull-ups on a tree branch, leg lunges off a big log, and military presses with heavy rocks while marching in place are perfect examples of how to turn the outdoors into a great gym.

Cool-Down and Meditation

Cool down by slowing your pace and easing your intensity. Practice many of the same movements you performed in the warm-up. Slow your walk to long strides and arm swings. This point in your workout is a great time to perform some tai chi exercises (see chapter 4) to improve range of motion, enhance fluidity of movement, and strengthen body alignment and posture. Tai chi focuses on enhancing your body-mind connection: strengthening the mental connection or focus on your body's energy and on nature. It is an excellent way to warm up or cool down. Finally, take the time also to enhance flexibility by practicing static stretching, holding stretches for 30 to 40 seconds. Focus on stretching the chest and upper back, lower back, hip flexors, gluteals, hamstrings, adductors, calves, and tibiales, as these are primary movers of rugged walking (see chapter 4 for stretches). Complete the workout session with a three- to five-minute meditation. Find a cool, quiet spot. Sit still with your eyes closed for several moments while breathing deeply. Concentrate on following the breath in and out. Sense your body calming down and relaxing (see chapter 8 for meditation techniques).

Exercise Programs for Rugged Walkers

This section presents rugged walker programs for beginner, intermediate, and advanced levels of fitness. Each program builds upon the skills and fitness level of the program before it. The following charts present an outline of the duration, rating of perceived exertion (see chapter 2), and description of the exercises for each segment of the workout. This will give you some idea of how the rugged walking workouts are designed.

Some people may want to do the rugged walking workout everyday, but others may not. How often during the week you do the program will depend on your fitness level and goals. Some may use the program as their main exercise regime, while others may choose to do it every now and then as part of their fitness routine. Whatever your exercise regime, it is recommended that you exercise a minimum of three times per week to ensure conditioning benefits. However, what is most important is that you do as many workouts a week as feel comfortable and that you do not pressure yourself into doing more if this causes you great inconvenience or stress. Quite simply, any exercise at all is better than none. If you do choose to workout almost every day, be sure to give yourself at least one day of rest in every week. This is a good day to stretch, relax, and meditate. This helps the body and mind recover and be replenished so that you do not become overworked but instead are invigorated for the next workout.

Each program level has moderate and intense workouts to provide you with guidance to work more intensely on some days than on others but within your level of fitness. It is recommended that you alternate your moderate and intense workouts. This will help you progress through one program level and advance to the next. Your progression from beginner to intermediate to advanced level will depend entirely on how fit you feel and what your goals are. If you are just beginning an exercise program or learning fitness walking, you may want to start with the beginner program. If you are an advanced exerciser, however, you may want to start with the intermediate or advanced program.

If you are a beginner, your program should begin with easier and more moderate activities until your body has time to experience the training benefits and is strong enough to progress. It takes time for your body to condition and adapt to the increasing energy demands placed on it by exercise. The training effect—becoming stronger both in your cardiorespiratory and muscular systems— occurs differently for different people and depends directly on how consistently and how hard you exercise. When and how to progress is easy to determine. Many fitness professionals recommend that you increase the duration and intensity of your workout by approximately 5 to 10 percent each week. But there is really no magic formula, and the rate of progression should be particular to you. There is no exact period of time that you should remain at a certain program level. Some people may remain at one level for a long time, while others may advance to the next program level within four to six weeks. If you are enjoying where you are and do not feel the need to change your program, then continue to work at your current level. If you feel the level has become too easy and less motivating, this is a good indication that you should advance your program. Trust your body. It will instinctively want to increase the intensity of the workout as you become more conditioned, and it will want to ease up if you are overdoing it.

Progression for you may mean increasing your frequency and becoming more consistent: getting out there a bit more often and exercising regularly. It may mean longer workouts or increasing your intensity (how hard you exercise). You can increase the intensity of your workout easily by adding one or all of the following: more intervals of the same drills, longer intervals of the same drills, same drills on more rugged terrain (i.e., uphill), same intervals plus more advanced drills, longer intervals plus more advanced drills. In any case, you have control, and you will know what to do and when to do it.

The beginner program is designed to get you started easily on an exercise program. The focus is to learn proper walking and speed techniques so that walking becomes an effective fitness activity for you. This program also helps you get used to walking off-road on rugged terrain. The intermediate program begins to advance your fitness level by using both speed (see chapter 3) and terrain drill (see chapter 5) interval-training techniques. The intermediate level also integrates muscle-conditioning circuits and tai chi exercises for enhancing your flexibility and your body-mind connection. Tai chi exercises are presented in chapter 4. The advanced program is designed to present a very tough, challenging workout. It encourages a high level of self-motivation to push you through very advanced speed and terrain drills. This program is for individuals who have an advanced level of fitness and who want to push to their limit. It is also designed to awaken your wild energy and to motivate you to really go for it!

Beginning Rugged Walker: Going Off-Road

This level focuses on getting you used to walking as a fitness activity as well as to walking on off-road terrain. Getting used to this terrain is important because it does elicit a very different physical sensation from walking on-road, and if you are not comfortable with where you are walking, you will be distracted from your workout. Off-road or rugged terrain can be dangerous if you have not exercised on it before. It may feel soft and slippery, and therefore you feel less stable until you get the hang of it. Your fitness goal in this level is to master proper walking posture and speed techniques while on rugged terrain. You also want to work up to exercising at least three times per week. I recommend that as a beginner you work out at the moderate level for your first four to six weeks of training before you advance on to the intense workout. In the intense level, you begin to practice interval training by practicing speed walking, which will increase your intensity.

◆ Moderate Workout (35 Minutes) ◆

Introducing Proper Walking and Body-Mind Techniques

Segment	Duration	RPE	Activity
Warm-up	10 min	10-12	Relaxed, brisk walking; rhythmic stretching; breathing deeply.
Aerobics	15 min	12-14	Faster brisk walking on flat terrain, first on-road then off-road. Practice proper walking and body-mind techniques.
Cool-down	8 min	10-12	Slow down to relaxed, brisk walking, and follow with rhythmic and then static stretching (primarily for hip flexors, quadriceps, hamstrings, upper and lower back, chest, calves, and shins).
Meditation	2 min	6-7	Sit quietly, eyes closed, and focus on your breathing and your body.

◆ Intense Workout (45 Minutes) ◆

Introducing Speed Intervals

Segment	Duration	RPE	Activity
Warm-up	10 min	10-12	Relaxed, brisk walking; rhythmic stretching; breathing deeply.
Aerobics	25 min	12-14	Faster walking pace, mostly on flat rugged terrain.
		15-17	Add some hills or an interval or two of speed walking.
Cool-down	8 min	10-12	Slow down to brisk walking, and follow with rhythmic and then static stretching (primarily for hip flexors, quadriceps, hamstrings, upper and lower back, chest, calves, and shins).
Meditation	2 min	6-7	Sit quietly, eyes closed, and focus on your breathing and your body.

Intermediate Rugged Walker: Moving Ahead

At the intermediate level you begin to feel more fit and therefore more confident of your physical abilities to move ahead. This level introduces the 18 terrain drills (see chapter 5). At this level you work through more interval training, using terrain drills, and begin muscle-conditioning circuit training, all of which will cause you to use more of your body in different ways than at the beginner level. This will help you gain greater fitness and greater awareness of the sensations of your body (body-mind connection). As you learn the terrain drills, for this level of intensity use those that feel relatively comfortable and not too strenuous. Allow yourself time to get used to the feel of the movement before you try to perform it with greater intensity (e.g., with greater speed, larger range of motion, or higher jump). In addition to the terrain drills you will also add agility and balance drills. Tai chi exercises for enhanced body-mind connection, flexibility, and balance and fluidity of movement are also introduced in this level. Although this program provides you with a more intense workout than the beginner program, you may also want to increase your exercise frequency from three to perhaps five days.

◆ Moderate Workout (45 Minutes) ◆

Introducing Terrain Drills and Tai Chi Exercises

Segment	Duration	RPE	Activity
Warm-up	10 min	10-12	Relaxed, brisk walking; rhythmic stretching; breathing deeply.
Aerobics	20 min	12-14	Faster-paced walking.
		15-17	Interval training: Add several speed and terrain drill intervals. Be sure to keep the terrain drills at a moderate level of intensity.

Segment	Duration	RPE	Activity
Tai chi	5 min	10-12	This segment is optional. First cool down somewhat from the aerobic training by returning to relaxed, brisk walking. Choose one or two of the tai chi movements from chapter 4 to loosen up and feel fluid. Focus on performing these exercises with fluidity.
Cool-down	8 min	10-12	If you performed tai chi, move on to static stretching (primarily of hip flexors, quadriceps, hamstrings, upper and lower back, chest, calves, and shins). If you did not do tai chi, slow to a relaxed, brisk walk, and follow with rhythmic and then static stretching.
Meditation	2 min	6-7	Sit quietly, eyes closed, and focus on your breathing and your body.

♦ Intense Workout (60 Minutes) ♦

Introducing Muscle-Conditioning Circuits and Balance and Agility Drills

Segment	Duration	RPE	Activity
Warm-up	10 min	10-12	Relaxed, brisk walking; rhythmic stretching; breathing deeply.
Aerobics	35 min	12-14	Fast-paced walking.
		15-17	Interval training: Add several speed and terrain drill intervals. Try performing some of the drills with more intensity. Intersperse with muscle-conditioning circuits using manual resistance or light free weights (rocks, logs, resistance band, etc.).

Continued on next page

Segment	Duration	RPE	Activity
		12-14	As you are cooling down from the interval and circuit training, add balance and agility drills, such as log walking, balancing on rocks, climbing trees, climbing over rocks, straddle-jumping streams—play with the terrain.
Tai chi	5 min	10-12	This segment is optional. First cool down somewhat from the aerobic training by returning to relaxed, brisk walking. Choose one or two of the tai chi movements from chapter 4 to loosen up and feel fluid. Focus on performing these exercises with fluidity.
Cool-down	7 min	10-12	If you performed tai chi, move on to static stretching (primarily of hip flexors, quadriceps, hamstrings, upper and lower back, chest, calves, and shins). If you did not do tai chi, slow to a relaxed, brisk walk, and follow with rhythmic and then static stretching.
Meditation	3 min	6-7	Sit quietly, eyes closed, and focus on your breathing and your body.

Advanced Rugged Walker: Go for It!

This level focuses on a very advanced workout. Now that you have mastered the basic techniques of proper walking and speed and have practiced some terrain drills, muscle-conditioning circuits, balance and agility drills, and tai chi exercises, you are ready to go for it! You should make certain that you are careful and safe, but really let yourself sweat and get out of breath. Take your workout to tougher terrain: steeper hills; longer, steeper stairs; soft, sandy beaches. Make your workout tougher by performing each drill with greater intensity (faster, bigger range of motion, higher leaps and jumps). Even feel your muscles burn in some of the exercises. Be adventurous and allow yourself to be spontaneous with the terrain. Create your own drills and other conditioning exercises and intervals using anything you can find in your environment. You may also want to make your program more advanced by working out more frequently, perhaps five or six days a week. To create some variety, plan a long, long trek—10 miles or so—once a month through a forest preserve or along a beach. This will help you plan a goal for your training and see how it feels to meet a challenge.

◆ Moderate Workout (60 Minutes) ◆

Working on Tougher Terrain and Using More Advanced Drills and Muscle-Conditioning Exercises

Segment	Duration	RPE	Activity
Warm-up	10 min	10-12	Relaxed, brisk walking; rhythmic stretching; breathing deeply.
Aerobics	35 min	12-14	Faster-paced walking.
		15-17	Interval training: Several speed and terrain drill intervals on very rugged terrain (e.g., steep hills, over obstacles, up stairs, in the sand). Intersperse with advanced muscle-conditioning circuits (e.g., squats, deep lunges, and upper-body exercises using greater resistance, such as resistance bands, weights, rocks, logs, or your body's weight against trees).
		12-14	As you are cooling down from the interval and circuit training, add balance and agility drills, such as log walking, balancing on rocks, climbing trees, climbing over rocks, straddle-jumping streams—play with the terrain.

Continued on next page

Segment	Duration	RPE	Activity
Tai chi	5 min	10-12	This segment is optional. First cool down somewhat from the aerobic training by returning to relaxed, brisk walking. Choose one or two of the tai chi movements from chapter 4 to loosen up and feel fluid. Focus on performing these exercises with fluidity.
Cool-down	7 min	10-12	If you performed tai chi, move on to static stretching (primarily of hip flexors, quadriceps, hamstrings, upper and lower back, chest, calves, and shins). If you did not do tai chi, slow to a relaxed, brisk walk, and follow with rhythmic and then static stretching. Stretches may be more advanced and held for a longer period.
Meditation	3 min	6-7	Sit quietly, eyes closed, and focus on your breathing and your body.

◆ Intense Workout (75 Minutes) ◆

The Longest, Toughest Workout

Segment	Duration	RPE	Activity
Warm-up	7 min	10-12	Relaxed, brisk walking; rhythmic stretching; breathing deeply.
Aerobics	50 min	12-14	Fast-paced walking.
		15-17	Interval training: Speed and advanced terrain drill intervals on rugged terrain—more climbing and advanced hiking, interspersed with your favorite, most intense terrain drills and muscle-conditioning circuits (e.g., squats and advanced upper-body exercises with heavy resistance). Get intense!

Segment	Duration	RPE	Activity
		12-14	As you are cooling down from the interval and circuit training, add balance and agility drills, such as log walking, balancing on rocks, climbing trees, climbing over rocks, straddle-jumping streams—play with the terrain.
Tai chi	5 min	10-12	This segment is optional. First cool down somewhat from the aerobic training by returning to relaxed, brisk walking. Choose one or two of the tai chi movements from chapter 4 to loosen up and feel fluid. Focus on performing the more advanced movements with fluidity. Practice the movements more slowly for more power and balance.
Cool-down	8 min	10-12	If you performed tai chi, move on to static stretching (primarily of hip flexors, quadriceps, hamstrings, upper and lower back, chest, calves, and shins). If you did not do tai chi, slow to a relaxed, brisk walk, and follow with rhythmic and then static stretching. Stretches may be more advanced and held for a longer period.
Meditation	5 min	6-7	Sit quietly, eyes closed, and focus on your breathing and your body.

CHAPTER
7

Staying On Course

Getting started and staying on course with your own fit and healthy lifestyle is much easier than you may think. It merely takes a little forethought about what you enjoy and a little time to put a program together. The following information will walk you through the steps of designing an individualized lifestyle program and provide tips to help you stay on course.

A new "walk" of life means a new way of life. It is important to realize that making lifestyle changes is not a program you embark on merely for a while, but rather is a commitment fulfilled throughout your lifetime. You know that things worth having take commitment and patience. You also know a healthy, happy you is the most valuable thing there is in life. The first step in designing a fitness program is to acknowledge that you are body, mind, and spirit, and it is vitally important to integrate physical, mental, and emotional/spiritual exercises into your program. Without giving attention to each aspect of who you are, your overall constitution is weakened. Relating this to the concept of reciprocating influences, if one aspect of who you are (for example, your physical self) is given attention, this will provide enriching energy and support for the other aspects that make you who you are (your mental and emotional selves). When you exercise, you feel mentally more alert and emotionally more confident. You feel better able to deal with stress. By neglecting one aspect of who you are, for example, your physical self, you feel mentally and emotionally drained. Your self-confidence and self-esteem are lower. When you take care of yourself physically, mentally, and emotionally, you have much more to give to yourself and to others.

We understand how important good health and fitness are to our sense of fulfillment and happiness. However, most people have a hard time getting started and staying with an ongoing fitness and healthy lifestyle program. Fitness professionals are finding that after 15 years of the "fitness boom" 90 percent of the adult population is still not exercising on a regular basis. Nor are adults eating well and relaxing. These results may have something to do with perceptions. How you perceive exercise and nutrition affects whether or not you exercise and eat well. It affects how you design your fitness program. How you design your fitness program significantly influences your motivation and whether or not you will keep exercising and eating well on a regular basis.

Adherence to an exercise program feels difficult when you perceive exercise as too complicated and uncomfortable. The way to "fit in" to the fitness movement for many people is too expensive (joining a club, buying exercise clothes), too embarrassing (styles of clothes, ability to exercise), or too stressful (making time to exercise, trying to fulfill an exercise prescription of, say, 30-minute sessions three times per week, feeling guilty for not exercising). A commitment to eating well is challenging for people for whom "eating well" means "go on a diet." Diets feel rigid, denying ourselves what we enjoy eating, so most people feel deprived and eventually go back to their old ways of eating.

Many people believe that making lifestyle changes for a healthier, happier life and sticking to them is not easy. We tend to make it difficult by making very extreme and dramatic choices in what we try to change. Our focus often is on making our bodies "perfect": thin and well-toned. We may believe that if we manipulate our bodies to the point that we are satisfied with them, we will finally be happy. This approach is overwhelming from the start, with its impossible tasks of the "hard-body" workout and highly restrictive diets, which only result in making us feel deprived, disappointed, and discouraged into giving up.

You do not have to run the marathon or "pump iron" like Arnold Schwarzenegger to be healthy and fit, to look and feel good. A very healthy and fit lifestyle does not have to be a life-long *challenge.* Rather, it can be a lifelong *enjoyment.* But this takes a change in perspective: a change from idolizing the "perfect" body to the desire for better physical and emotional well-being.

◘ Being healthy and fit is as easy as taking a walk in the great outdoors.

The following guidelines are offered to help you reflect on a new perspective from which to create a healthier, happier lifestyle. They are intended to encourage you to be more self-motivated, which will significantly ease the process of change.

Take Responsibility: You're Worth It

This may sound strange, but I believe many of our unhealthy habits come from an underlying belief that we do not deserve a better life—that we deserve to struggle and are not worth the effort. I also believe that we can change our beliefs by taking responsibility and deciding we are worth it. Only you have the power to make your life what you want it to be. The fact you are reading this book is a strong indication that you feel you are worth it. Congratulations! You have just taken the first and most difficult step toward a more fulfilling life.

It seems that those who have been successful in making healthy lifestyle changes have this belief—that they are worth it—and therefore they are self-motivated. Highly motivated people decide to take charge of their lives: deciding what to eat, how to exercise, how to work, how to play, how to relax—what habits they want to live with to make themselves feel good. Their motivation comes from a commitment to be healthier and happier people, from a commitment to themselves. They are willing to make time for themselves to experience the physical and emotional strengthening that comes from a healthy, fit lifestyle. They do not allow themselves to make excuses. This self-nurturing lifestyle further strengthens their self-esteem. Highly motivated people have a positive outlook on life. They are better able to deal with stress because they have a high level of self-confidence, which comes from strong self-esteem. Highly motivated people choose to search for ways to give themselves more things that are healthy and enjoyable rather than for ways to deny themselves things they enjoy and are told are "bad" for them. For example, with regard to weight loss, they do not focus as much on how they look and on counting calories to keep weight off for the "perfect" body, but instead focus more on ways to eat well so they feel healthier. They choose to see exercise not as a "workout" but as playing and having fun.

Highly motivated people are made. They are not necessarily born that way. You can become a highly self-motivated person by finding your motivation through a healthier perspective. This perspective is found in a commitment to nurture yourself, from a belief that you are worth it. It takes concentration and practice to cultivate a new perspective and self-motivation. Motivation comes from the feeling of success. Find small changes that work for you. A few small, simple changes add up to a new way of life. Allow yourself to feel good when you accomplish them. Notice how good you feel physically and emotionally after you exercise, after you eat well. When you integrate changes that you are likely to accomplish and that feel good, your tendency to find excuses is much less. Be sure to treat yourself with compassion so that you do not succumb to the demotivation of self-judgment if you happen to miss a workout or eat something fattening. Perceive each day as a new beginning, rather than criticizing yourself for past mistakes. It is also important to give yourself time for new behaviors to become habits. It takes practice and patience. I have heard that it takes approximately 6 months or so of consistent practice for new changes to become lifestyle behaviors.

Have Fun

Research has demonstrated that *diets* and *exercise prescriptions* do not seem to work on a long-term basis. Why? I believe it is because they are not fun. Having fun is a very basic human need. We sometimes allow ourselves to become so busy and stressed that we are distracted from ourselves, distracted from the fact that we are not having any fun. We have come to trust more in the advice of others and what they tell us to do rather than in our own inner knowing. We rarely follow our instincts, our natural inner guidance, which would tell us that the way to greater well-being is through healthy pleasures (*Healthy Pleasures,* Robert Ornstein, PhD & David Sobel, MD, Reading, M., Addison-Wesley Publishing, 1989). If we are going to be successful at making healthy lifelong changes, then we need to make certain we enjoy them. I think we learn faster when we are having fun. Allow yourself to play more and have fun. When you are having fun, you are relaxed and open. The reduction of stress prevents the wear and tear on your body and your mind. You laugh more often, which is a great lift to the spirit as well as to the abdominals. You tend to be more active, to do such things as dancing, playing a game with the kids, riding a bike, or taking a walk with friends—very effective ways of conditioning the body and mind. When you are having fun, you eat in a more relaxed fashion. You eat less and focus more clearly on your choices of food, eating delicious, healthy foods. Often you will choose less high-fat foods as these tend to be the food of choice when we are stressed and feel we need some nurturing.

Maximize the things you enjoy doing and minimize those you do not. Things you enjoy doing will easily become a part of your lifestyle. It is easy to think of ways to make life more enjoyable if you are willing to take a moment for yourself and allow your body and mind to share with you. Trust in the messages you hear. Your body will guide you to what is best. In the pursuit of "healthy pleasures," you enjoy life. When you enjoy life, you are more healthy and fit.

Be More Active and Exercise

The research is in! Being physically active can definitely help you feel happier, look better, and perform more easily. Our modern lifestyle is one in which the mind is very active but the body and the spirit have been ignored and neglected. The body and spirit are sedentary and beginning to atrophy, to lose their strength and power. Modern conveniences have helped habituate us to physical inactivity, and the pace and values of modern society have suppressed the spirit. When you lead an active life, you feel happier and more confident. As the conditioning continues, the body adapts in ways you feel good about: becoming stronger, leaner, more agile, more capable, healthier. Your body feels good, so you feel good. This gives a great lift to the spirit and thus is a tremendous motivator in helping you stay on course.

Being more active and exercising helps you stay younger and healthier. Exercising has been shown to be a major method of preventing heart disease, cardiovascular disease (lowering blood pressure and raising levels of HDL "good" cholesterol), obesity, osteoporosis, depression, physical injury, poor posture, back pain, and stress, and effectively delays the process of aging (one of my favorite benefits). Exercise is the key component to permanent weight loss. The activity itself burns calories (the amount depends on the frequency, intensity, and duration of the workout), and activity is thought to contribute 10 to 30 percent of your daily caloric expenditure. More important, however, exercise helps to maintain and increase muscle mass, the energy-consuming tissue of your body. Your muscle mass is thought to contribute 60 percent of your total caloric expenditure. The more conditioned muscle you have, the higher your resting metabolic rate.

Even with all these known benefits of exercise, however, something often gets in the way of committing to exercising on a regular basis. For some, it may be expecting too much too soon; impatience therefore discourages them from continuing. Others may have chosen a program that they cannot easily and conveniently adhere to, and therefore it becomes a hassle rather than an enjoyable experience. Others may push too hard too fast so that soreness inhibits them from going on. Still others believe they do not have the time (a big excuse for most of us). Keep in mind that you may overcome all these excuses if you are willing to make a commitment to yourself. Your health and happiness depend on you.

Unfortunately, over the last decade some people have come to understand that exercise is a mandate for a very intense, hard workout in order to reap the benefits of conditioning, such as weight loss and better health. However, the experts all agree that low- to moderate-intensity activity done frequently (several times a day or once a day for a relatively long period of time) is most effective for weight loss as well as fitness and health. You do not have to be in pain to gain, (or lose weight, as the case may be). Exercising does not have to be hard or uncomfortable. Your body instinctively loves to be active: to run, dance, walk—*to play.* You are a muscular and respiratory being, after all. When you choose the type of exercise or activity to integrate into your lifestyle, it is important that you begin with something you enjoy. Doing something you enjoy has not only many physiological benefits, but significant psychological benefits as well. It picks up your mood, and you are likely to exercise longer and more regularly. Give yourself credit for daily activity. It is exercise too. Taking walks outside alone or with a friend, gardening and yard work, riding a bike, walking the dog or walking to the store, hiking nature trails, and rigorously cleaning your home are all exercise activities.

Eat Well and In Moderation

Eating well is not as complicated or as unenjoyable as you may have believed. The formula for losing weight is rather simple. However, for many of us it is not easy to do. It may sound strange, but the first thing you need to consider for losing weight or eating well is to look at your relationship with food. Most of us do not know how to eat *in moderation* or strictly in response to our biological needs. We eat mostly to indulge in the taste and to satisfy emotional needs. This is not necessarily bad, but it is may lead us to excessive eating. You probably have a favorite food, such as chocolate chip cookies or ice cream. There is no biological need for these foods; you just enjoy a "treat" every now and then. If you do not allow yourself these foods from time to time, they become an obsession. Then when you do finally break down and allow yourself to eat them, you usually eat much more than you would have if you'd let yourself have it in the first place. Therefore, it may be best to eat what you want but eat it in moderation. It has been my experience that mastering moderation is a much more enjoyable and healthy way to live than always depriving myself of chocolate chip cookies.

We all want to be thin; it's a symptom of our culture. In our quest to lose weight we look for lots of information that can lead us to "success," and in our rush for living we usually look for the "quick fix." But experience tells us that the quick fix or diet does not lead to better lifelong eating habits. Quick weight-loss plans do not teach realistic eating behaviors, but rather help people lose weight through specifically prepared and highly restrictive meal plans. Diets that require special planning, unusual foods, involved or complicated preparation, or extra expense make it almost impossible to adopt this type of eating as a lifelong behavior. You may do it for a while because you see it as a worthwhile goal, but you will eventually end up feeling unsatisfied, even resentful, for having to go through such a struggle and thus return to your old, unhealthy ways. When your diet is over, you are not quite sure how to eat to maintain your new weight, and you usually put the weight back on. You are once again physically and emotionally heavy and eventually go back on the diet. The process becomes much more complicated, difficult, and expensive than it needs to be. A guiding principle to managing weight is to keep the process simple and sensible: simply *eat well and in moderation;* and get plenty of exercise.

◆ Eating well and in moderation are important for our well-being.

Eat less fat, more fiber, moderate complex carbohydrates, fewer dairy products, low protein, and lots of variety. Drink plenty of water. Creating healthy eating habits by modifying what you already like to eat is a guarantee to success. Drastically changing how you eat, by going on a fad diet for example, will be extremely difficult and last only a short while. By modifying what you already like to eat, adding changes and new foods in small ways, the process is gradual, and you continue to feel satisfied. You are not constantly trying to deny yourself things to eat, but rather deciding to try something new. Your gradual, smaller changes lead to larger changes, and eventually you will see how drastically your eating habits have changed over time. You will marvel at how easy it was.

It is very easy to follow a low-fat eating strategy because this type of eating is very satisfying. The typical American has simply gotten used to high-fat tastes. By cutting back gradually on these types of foods and trying other foods instead, such as more complex-carbohydrate food—fruits, vegetables, grains—your tastes will gradually change. Simply avoiding high-fat food will itself result in a reduction of calories. Fat has nine calories per gram, compared with four calories per gram for carbohydrate or protein. By exchanging high-fat food for other types of food, you provide the body with food of greater nutritional value and with energy sources more easily metabolized than fat. Keep in mind, though, that excess food, whether fat or carbohydrate or protein, will be converted by the body to be stored as fat. Remember: *moderation.*

Cutting the fat in your diet means being more aware of where it is and gradually exchanging these foods for other things to eat. Read labels and choose foods that are less than 30 percent fat (recommended by the American Heart Association) or that are approximately 3 grams of fat (or 27 fat calories) for each 100 total calories. Purchase minimally processed foods. Change the combination of things you eat: less meat, more vegetables and grains. Look for something quick to eat in the produce section of your market rather than a fast-food restaurant. Check out the new, great-tasting, low-fat munchies on the market, and change to low-fat dressings. You can probably think of many more ways of reducing the fat in your diet.

Fiber and water are critical to healthy eating and a happy disposition. Not to be rude, but being regular helps me remain healthier and happier. Elimination is the natural detoxifying process of the body. Constipation can cause headaches, nausea, and irritability. If you do not eliminate regularly, you may be more prone to diseases such as colon cancer, irritable bowel syndrome, and poor skin. Walking is a great antidote to irregularity.

There are not really any *bad* foods. But there are bad, or rather *unhealthy,* behaviors. Excess instead of moderation is usually what gets you into trouble with eating poorly and gaining weight. The American culture functions at a high level of intensity, and it can be challenging to function in a moderate manner. However, moderation is truly the key to health, fitness, and well-being. A daily relaxation and meditation practice will help you slow down and focus in. You will make healthier choices from this calmer perspective. And remember, each day is a new opportunity. If you have been able to stay with your new eating habits, it is another day to celebrate and to continue on with your success. If you have not been able stick to your modifications as much as you would have liked, it is another opportunity to have compassion and forgive yourself. Nothing has been lost because only today counts.

 ## Undoing Weight Loss Myths

It is very important that we ask ourselves: why are we going on these diets anyway? Some of us want to look better in our jeans, and there is nothing wrong with that. But are we trying to lose weight because we want to be healthier or because we are worshipping the "perfect body" image? Some people worship this false idol, and it is costing them their health and happiness. They often go on drastic diets that result in low energy and susceptibility to illness. Some people abuse themselves with the "quick fix" because it is what they believe they are supposed to do; it is the social norm. Treating oneself this way comes from low self-esteem. We may believe that we need to go on drastic diets and extreme eating habits to fit in and be accepted. It is time to treat our body with respect and allow it to be the way it needs to be by giving it a chance to be healthy and natural. We need to give up the guilt of not having a "perfect" body. If you are good to your body, it will be kind in return. One of the wonderful things about deciding to be more active and to live a healthier and happier lifestyle is that you usually lose weight, become more fit, and feel happier more permanently. We are what we believe we are. We are how we treat ourselves, and how we treat ourselves comes from what we think and feel about ourselves. What we think and feel about ourselves comes from what we were taught growing up. We can undo unhealthy myths and create new beliefs.

Relax and Meditate

You have experienced stress in your life, and you know how it affects your body and mind: making you feel ill and very unhappy. Too much uncontrolled stress wears you out. It makes you tired, interferes with your health and fitness, and has a great impact on the quality of your life.

Every person has a different capacity for stress. Some people require more stress than others to be happy and well-adjusted biologically and emotionally. However, it seems that everyone at some time or another allows stress to get the better of them. It is necessary that you learn techniques that will help you manage stress. The first key step is to learn *awareness* of your body when it is experiencing stress. Your body is your primary barometer of how much stress is in your life. You may at times let your mind rationalize the stress and ignore that your body is feeling tense and ill. Honoring the body by learning how to listen to it will give you clues to sense how you are feeling about what is happening in your life. Then, if you choose, you may look more deeply into the causes of your stress. At any rate, being aware of how your body feels gives you the opportunity to change the impact stress has on your body and in your life.

Learning how to listen to the body takes practice. In our busy, hectic lives, we have forgotten how to be truly quiet, truly alone and internally focused. We are continually distracted from our bodies. Meditation gives you the opportunity to focus in on and listen to your body and your heart. A simple meditation practice of spending a few quiet moments of deep, relaxed breathing immediately relieves both physical and emotional stress. Meditating each day provides a strong foundation for greater peace in your life as you gain more resiliency to better cope with stress. Chapter 8 presents more detail on the impact of stress and the benefits of meditation.

The Moment Is Now: Take Stock in Yourself

There is no time like the present to get started on a healthier lifestyle: take responsibility, have more fun, exercise, eat well and in moderation, and relax and meditate. The following thought exercise is designed to help you get in touch with yourself and practice feeling the perspective that you deserve to be fit, healthy, and happy. Often we close ourselves off from life's glorious, endless possibilities by limiting our personal growth with excuses. Perhaps the following inventory will help you to begin to develop in a new direction. You will evaluate your current habits, set goals and processes, and make new plans so that you will feel motivated about staying on course.

1. Take stock in yourself.

Sit back, take a breath, relax, and let your thoughts and feelings settle down. This is the most important step in the process of goal setting. It is important to begin your process of goal setting from a positive perspective of yourself. So be proud and take stock in yourself: think about and feel the happiness and satisfaction of all the wonderful and positive things about yourself—about who you are and what you have accomplished—no matter how insignificant they seem. Congratulate yourself: you deserve it. You have accomplished some terrific things. Write these down.

_____

_____

_____

_____

_____

_____

_____

_____

_____

_____

_____

2. Run wild and have fun.

Let your mind run wild, and think about all the things that you would like to be, to have, and to accomplish. Get in touch with your dreams and don't hold back. Let your creativity and imagination run wild. Tap into your spirit. Choose changes that involve every part of you: body, mind, and spirit. Consider and choose changes that are fun, affordable, convenient, and can be integrated easily into your daily lifestyle. Write down things that you really find fun, both things you have done before and new things you would like to try. Write these down. You will need good health and fitness to accomplish these goals. So now focus on your health and fitness goals and write these down.

_____

_____

_____

_____

_____

_____

_____

_____

_____

_____

_____

_____

3. Turn goals into processes.

Small changes turn into lifelong habits. You will most likely find that you are more successful at achieving your goals if you focus on the *process* of achieving your goal rather than on the goal itself. Break your goals down into smaller goals or steps. The only way you can walk through life is to take it one step at a time. Take each goal and break it down into at least three smaller ones. Of these three smaller steps, consider which ones you may realistically be able to accomplish in a week, in a day. If some will take longer, break them down further, if possible.

For example, losing weight is a goal that is often very overwhelming because the expectation is to lose 20 pounds in a week. From a healthy approach, your body should lose no more than approximately two pounds a week. Begin by focusing only on the next thing you are going to eat, and decide whether you really want to eat it. There is an immediate sense of control over what you eat, and this has an immediate impact on your weight. As other examples, learning to exercise regularly may begin with a walk around the block tonight after dinner. Learning to reduce stress by meditating may be an overwhelming goal if you have decided that you are going to start out by meditating 30 minutes each day. Break this down. Sit quietly and breathe deeply for 30 seconds each day. When you are ready, gradually increase the time.

Write down your three smaller goals for each of your main goals.

_____

_____

_____

_____

_____

_____

_____

_____

_____

_____

4. Keep a journal.

Keep a daily, weekly, and monthly checklist of what is happening. It is an excellent way to heighten your awareness of the choices you are making, of your habits, and of where you are and where you are going. This is meant to be a tool of self-awareness to help keep you on track, not for self-criticism. If this turns into a reminder of how much you have *not* accomplished, stop using it. Write down the changes you have made so far.

_____

_____

_____

_____

_____

_____

_____

_____

_____

5. Develop a support system.

Support yourself with compassion and surround yourself with friends. Surrounding yourself with positive feedback is very essential to your success. Surround yourself at work and at home with relationships with those who share your interests and ideas. Write down the names of people with whom you want to exercise or from whom you would like support in eating well. Go ask them.

_____

_____

_____

_____

_____

_____

6. Reward yourself.

Reward is a great motivator. Congratulate yourself for every little change you accomplish. No matter how small it may seem, it is a terrific accomplishment. A walk around a block is the beginning of your commitment to exercise. People tend to be so critical of themselves. Why not try being more complimentary instead? Write down what you have accomplished and how you will reward yourself. If you haven't accomplished anything yet, reward yourself anyway for being just who you are.

_____

_____

_____

_____

_____

_____

_____

_____

_____

7. Have compassion for yourself.

You will accomplish some goals more easily than others. Have patience with yourself when goals are more challenging. If you are kind to yourself, you will eventually achieve them. How can you be more compassionate toward yourself? Think of what you would say to someone else who feels the way you do to help them feel more positive and better supported. Write these down and say them to yourself.

_____

_____

_____

_____

_____

_____

_____

_____

8. Live in the moment.

The present moment (this moment right now) is the most important in your life. The past is over, and the future is not yet here. Make the most out of right now. Are you doing something you enjoy right now? This moment you are making changes for a better way of living by heightening your awareness about yourself. Write down how you feel right now, your emotions and sensations (focus on the sensations of your body in your chest and belly).

_____

_____

_____

_____

_____

_____

_____

9. Reassess and follow up.

Every now and then take a look at how things are going. Take a look at how close you are to your original goals, how your goals may have changed, and new goals you may have thought of. Be willing to be flexible and let goals go. Goals are your own creation, to be changed any time you wish. Be careful not to get so attached to a goal that you cause yourself great suffering while trying to accomplish it. Focusing intensely on goals may cause you to worry more about the future instead of enjoying the present. Goals that are best for you are ones that are relatively easy to accomplish. From time to time, write down any new goals, and walk yourself through steps 1 to 8 again.

Self-Care for the Rugged Walker

Rugged walking is a rigorous physical activity and results in significant physical tension that must be released through rest and relaxation to restore balance to the body. It is just as important to release the tension created by emotional stress to restore balance to the spirit. Life itself can feel like a more rigorous workout to the body than exercise does. You may know that it is important to release the stressful impact of exercise on your body, but you may be less aware about the impact of emotional stress on your body. This is evidence of the reciprocating influences between the body and the mind. Research now reveals that there is a direct relationship between our emotional and physical health and well-being. When you are stressed emotionally, you are stressed physically, and vice versa. Making decisions about your life while under stress usually generates more stress. The emotional stress of your life also has farther-reaching ramifications. It may feel overwhelming to realize that your personal stress influences world peace and the health of our planet, but it does. Personal stress affects how we treat ourselves, how we treat others, and how we treat the Earth. When we are stressed, so are others around us, creating more tension. Therefore, it is important to our personal and to our collective well-being not only to exercise, but to find time to rest and relax both physically and mentally.

In our fast-paced life of convenience and consumerism, we rarely find time to relax the "stress response." The problem seems to be that in today's world we very seldom give ourselves the opportunity or, more important, the permission to slow down, to attenuate our accelerating self. We have become workaholics and have forgotten how to relax and play. Without rest and recovery we eventually wear down and become susceptible to disease, illness, injury, anxiety, and depression. Without play we stifle our creative self. Without setting time aside to care for ourselves we become tired and lose our motivation: our motivation to exercise and eat well, our motivation for life. We are draining the vitality out of our life. We must either learn to reduce the stress in our lives or we are left facing the unhealthy and unhappy consequences.

The benefits of relaxation and meditation are very important to your health and well-being. They keep you young: physically and mentally flexible, creative, and open. Relaxation allows time for the body to slow down, easing the wear and tear that come from the stress both of exercise and of life experiences. During relaxation the body restores balance, rebuilds, and becomes stronger. Meditation restores balance of the mind and spirit. It allows time for the mind to slow down and for you to gain perspective, a sense of control and of resiliency to "bounce back" and face life's challenges.

There are many techniques that can help you relax and manage stress. Finding the method that is comfortable and enjoyable for you is most important to your success at integrating stress management into your life. Playing more often is a good way to start. When you play, you worry less and you laugh a lot, a response that induces tremendous relaxation and thus health benefits for your body and your mind. Gradually integrate into your life those activities that are quiet and that provide the opportunity to focus on yourself and your bodily sensations. Many people like to sit and listen to music or read a book, others like to take long walks, while others enjoy a massage. Many enjoy the more deep relaxation experience of meditation.

An excellent self-care program for rugged walkers is threefold, consisting of a series of stretching exercises for the whole body, a foot bath and body massage to help manage physical stress, and meditation to help manage emotional stress. A full-body stretching program is presented in chapter 4, and foot care, massage, and meditation techniques are presented in this chapter.

 Walk It

A flurry of activity. That's me. Rushing. Running.
Toward the future of becoming.
Away from the past of having been.
Where am I now . . . ?
Passing by life. Passing up the experience of now.
What am I missing . . . ?

Balance, harmony, rhythm, gentleness, compassion,
rapture, acceptance, calmness, awareness,
transformation, beauty, nature,
sun, sky, ocean, moon, mountain,
fulfillment, blessing, relaxation, peace,
happiness . . . these are my pursuits.

The rapture of living . . . "so that our life experiences
on the purely physical plane will have resonances within
our own innermost being and reality . . ."
says J.C.**

I will not hurry through living. Or I will miss it.
I will slow down.
I will erase the wear and tear of stress.
I will slow the accelerating thought patterns of my day.

Continued on next page

Walk It—continued

I will nurture my body and spirit by living
in the present moment.
I will realize every step I take.
Within the moment of each step
I will see all that is around me.
I will accept and cherish that which is nurturing
and change that which is not.
I will not drive my body down into gravity.
Rather I will lift up and float across it.
I will stop the negative self-talk
of all the "have tos" and "should nots".
I will be gentle with who it is that I am.
I will choose to do the things that make me happy
and leave the rest to others.
I will say good-bye to finding my self worth
in the eyes of others.
And I will risk getting to know my true inner self.

Take a deep breath.
Slow up a bit.
See the beauty of nature.
Feel the spirituality of life—the warmth of the sun,
the caress of the wind, the tingle of the rain,
the coolness of the forest, the security of a hug,
the ache of the tear, the arousal of the kiss.
Be the rapture of living.
Walk through life. Don't run.

**Joseph Campbell—*The Power of Myth*

Understanding Stress

In recent decades stress has become a serious health problem with significant negative impacts on the quality and longevity of life. Who wants to live long if they are unhealthy and unhappy? You know how it feels to be under stress. It is hard to focus, concentrate, and enjoy. You feel tired, weak, and insecure. Research tells us that over 85 percent of all diseases are stress related. Stress is a major risk factor for aging, injury, poor posture, aches and pains, poor mental and physical performance, and unhealthy habits and behaviors. Stress leads to unhappiness.

The best defense against the impact of stress is to understand it better. What really is stress? We have some idea, but let's take a closer look. Stress is the stimulus that motivates us to attain our life goals. This is called *eustress* and is not only a healthy, but also a necessary part of living. It stimulates us to strive, to achieve, to grow, to change. Without change there is no experience of living, no rapture, no life itself. Yet when change becomes too frequent or dramatic, it feels overwhelming and changes to *distress.* We tend to resist change in our lives somewhat because we often feel afraid of not knowing what will happen. This sense of fear and anxiety about the future generates our distress. It is important to notice that emotional stress is caused not so much by what is actually happening to us, but more by the fearful and negative things we think will happen. The point is that stress is essentially caused by our fearful thoughts which generate a certain attitude about life.

Emotional tension, a feeling of lack of control, and insecurity cause physical tension. Your body goes into overdrive. Adrenaline is produced, and respiration, heart rate, blood pressure, and muscle tension shoot up, all readying you for action: for "fight or flight." This *stress response,* when unreleased, manifests in the body as headaches, stiff neck, sore back, aching shoulders, colds, illness, disease. These physical manifestations arise most often when you are distracted by your thoughts, unaware of what is happening to your body in the moment. You may look for a "quick fix" and take drugs to mask the pain rather than look for the underlying cause. However, these discomforts and illnesses are great wake-up calls, reminding you to pay attention to your life and the thoughts and feelings you have about it.

Consider the impact on your body as the overload of stress and tension goes on, day after day. Your muscles contract against the stress, and if you never rest, your body fatigues, becomes sore, and eventually breaks down. If you have a habit of hunching your shoulders when stressed, for example, your shoulders will begin to maintain this posture. Over time this posture limits your range of movement and causes great stiffness and physical discomfort, to say nothing about the negative affect on your physical appearance. This stress leads to permanent postural deviations and predisposition to injury. Furthermore, your immune system is weakened. Much of your body's energy and the nutrients needed to protect your systems from disease are being burned to fuel this high-energy state of stress. You become ill.

Stress also interferes with a healthy metabolism. Your body may hold on to fat stores in response to feeling threatened, much as it does when you go on a "starvation" diet. If you are unaware of your body's muscular tension and resulting discomfort, you are almost certainly unaware of your body's true biological needs, such as for food, sleep, activity, and rest. You may eat and sleep in response to emotion rather than to your natural state of hunger and fatigue. You are not truly satisfied after you eat or rested after you sleep. When stressed, you eat unconsciously. You are not aware of what you ate, what it tasted like, when you actually felt satisfied, and whether you even really wanted or enjoyed what you ate. It is easy to understand why weight management then becomes a problem.

Managing Physical Stress

Our physical stress and tension negatively influence our outlook. Therefore, it is critical to find ways to release and manage this stress. Releasing physical tension has a definite positive effect on our emotional disposition. We all know how good it feels to stretch. This is one of the best ways to reduce physical tension. Whenever you feel tense, take a moment to reach out and stretch: reach your arms out in front, overhead, and out back. Perform easy rhythmic stretches for the neck, shoulders, back, hips and legs, no matter where you are. Whatever feels tight, loosen it up. Chapter 4 presents a series of stretches optimal for helping the rugged walker relax after a challenging workout. These stretches actually are ideal at any time.

There are other excellent techniques you can use to reduce physical stress. Turn your bathroom into a spa resort. A bath and facial and foot massage are easy and inexpensive to do on your own. Throw lemons or oatmeal into your bath. Candlelight and aromas induce many relaxing emotions and wonderful memories. Massage is an excellent body-mind technique for reducing stress. As various strokes release physical tension, the sensation helps the mind become quiet and calm. As our thoughts slow, the body relaxes further. This is a perfect example of the concept of reciprocating influences. Presented below are some ideas for releasing physical tension through foot, face, and neck massage. Perhaps these will help stimulate your creativity to come up with stress-reducing techniques that are ideal for you. Relax and enjoy!

Foot and Ankle Massage

We take our feet for granted. They carry all our burdens in life and yet we give them little attention. Our feet connect us with the energy of the Earth. They carry and support us on our life's journey. How we stand and walk through life depends on the health and happiness of our feet. Our feet are the foundation of our physical and emotional postures. If our foundation is weak and tired, there is little to build upon, little to hold us up. How our feet feel on any given day greatly affects our disposition and our attitude. And our attitude affects our response to life. If our feet are sore, our rugged walk becomes a great struggle, one in which we are distracted by our physical discomfort from all the beauty and wonders around us.

A foot and ankle massage is particularly important for rugged walkers. Happy, healthy feet mean a happy, healthy you. To keep your feet healthy and happy, you need to care for them, give them special attention. Give them good shoes and socks and treat them to a "spa" often. Here is a simple, 10-minute "spa treatment" and massage. While you are performing the massage, you may want to listen to relaxing music and surround yourself with soothing aromas (lavender is a great choice). As you experience the massage, be sure to maintain deep, full breathing to release tension and enhance the relaxation response.

A foot and ankle massage is one of the most effective ways to release stress from your whole body. Begin your foot therapy by gently cleaning your feet with lukewarm water and an invigorating soap or lotion. Follow with a pedicure. Oil is not needed for this massage. To begin your foot massage, take your foot in both hands. It may be easy to sit in a chair and take your foot in your lap. Or you may prefer to sit on the floor with your foot in front of you. Press your fingers into the sole with your thumbs resting on the top of the foot. Massage in small circles beginning at the heel and moving through the arch to your toes. Be sure to apply a good, deep pressure throughout and spend some time in each area. Spend more time if you feel soreness or tension. Massage around the ball of each toe. Massage each toe. Before moving to the next toe, give the pad of the toe a strong squeeze, pressing top

◘ A foot massage is important to the health of your feet and overall enjoyment of your rugged walk.

to bottom (nail to sole) and then side to side. Reach your hand over the top of your toes so that the palm of your hand is holding the soles of the toes. Gently pull the toes up and back toward your knee to stretch the arch. As you pull the toes backward, point the ball of your foot toward the floor. Now place the palm of your hand on the top of your toes, and curl the toes toward the floor.

Next, gently press your thumbs into the top of your foot, massaging from your toes toward your ankle. Work carefully and deeply over the midsection and around the ankle, from the top or front of the ankle around to the outside, then to the back, and then to the inside of the anklebone. Come behind the ankle and gently pinch the Achilles tendon and around the edge of the heel. Continue the massage up the ankle, into the calf and along the shin. Be sure to work longer in any particularly sore areas. Working acupressure points (pressing your fingers at various points) along the shinbone on both the inside and outside edges is very helpful in releasing tension and blocked energy. These points are considered to be along the energy meridian of the liver, kidneys, and adrenal glands.

Finally, flex the ankle (stretching the calf and Achilles tendon) and then point the foot and toes (stretching the tibialis, or shin, and the top midstep). Repeat flexing and pointing rhythmically several times. Then hold each stretch, a flex and a point, for 45 seconds. Gently circle the foot from the ankle in one direction and then in the other direction. Sit quietly for a moment and notice how this foot and ankle feel in comparison to the other one. Repeat this massage on the other foot.

 ## Foot Reflexology

Foot reflexology maps all the body's major organ, muscle, and skeletal systems to a particular corresponding area on the sole of the foot. For example, your neck corresponds to the neck of your big toe, your sinuses to the pads of each toe, your spine to the arch, and your heart near the ball of your foot. As you massage your feet and ankles, you massage your

Continued on next page

Foot Reflexology—continued

whole body. During your massage you may find that some areas in your foot are more sensitive than others. This may reveal a weakness, soreness, or health problem in one of your body's systems. For example, the arch of your foot may feel tired and sore, and you may realize that your back feels the same way. Massaging the arch of your foot will help ease tension in your back. There are a number of excellent full-body massage books on the market which will provide information as well as reference for reflexology.

Face and Neck Massage

As you are probably aware, your face and neck hold much of your tension. You may not realize how much until you take the time to massage your neck and feel the release. It is amazing how relaxing to our whole body a face and neck massage can feel. Find a position in which you feel most relaxed. Sitting in a chair with your feet flat on the floor should feel very comfortable. You will use both acupressure (pressing at various points) and circle massage (Swedish) techniques.

Begin your massage by gently pressing and circling your finger tips and thumbs around your scalp as if you were washing your hair. Begin at the back of the neck, come up through the back and over the top of your head, then move along the sides to your temples and around your ears. Press your fingertips into the midcenter of the forehead and massage out toward the temples. Finish each stroke with a little circle around the temple. Take your thumbs and press them into the top rim of your eye socket, beginning at the bridge of your nose and stroking along the rim toward the temple. Press your thumb gently in the corners of your eyes and with your eyes closed gently stroke outward over your eyelids, again toward the temples.

Gently press your fingers at the bridge of your nose and massage along the cheekbone outward to the temple. Massage the temple and work downward to the jawbone. Let your mouth open slightly as you massage at the joint and downward along the jaw. Finally, bring your thumbs to the center to your chin (you will need to invert your hands, palms up and elbows out front, to be able to place the thumbs at the center of your chin) and stroke outward along the jawbone toward your ears. Gently massage your ears by kneading them between your thumb and fingers. Continue to massage and use pressure-point technique (pressing your fingertips into points along the edges of the bone) around your ears, coming behind your ear and the back of your head toward the back of your neck. Continue to massage the back of your neck and out across the tops of your shoulders.

Place your fingers on the tops of your shoulders close to your neck, holding your elbows high and together in front of your nose. Press your fingers into your neck and shoulder area, and while pressing, pull your elbows down toward your chest. Your fingers will work deeply into the muscle as you pull your arms down. Work your fingers along your clavicle toward the front of your neck. Gently massage the front of the sides of your neck. Work gentle massage strokes down into your chest. Finish by gently placing your palms flat on your face, eyes closed. Take a deep, relaxing breath. Lie quietly for a moment, and sense how your face and head feel now.

Managing Emotional Stress

The first step in managing stress is to become aware of it and the affects it has on you. This takes reflection and exploration. Ask yourself: "What causes me stress?" Consider big issues or events as well as the details of your daily life. "How does stress affect me physically, mentally, and emotionally? What kind of things do I do when I am stressed out: eat, watch TV, yell, sleep? How do I feel: unhappy, demotivated, anxious?" Being *aware* of what causes you stress and how you feel and behave when you feel stressed allows you the opportunity to change the behavior and therefore the consequences. Emotional stress comes from the fear that we do not have control over our lives. There definitely are some very stressful changes in our lives such as death, divorce, family, relationship and job crises that we may not have direct control over.

However, we are able to control our perspective and attitude about them. The next step in managing your stress therefore is to observe your thoughts and your attitude. Do you tend to think positively or negatively about change, about your life? It is natural to have worries and regrets, but do you obsess about them? Since thoughts are your own creation, you have the power to change them, to change your attitude and perspective. And with a new perspective, a new attitude, you have the chance to change how you respond and behave.

The third step in managing stress is to learn to bring your thoughts "back home," out of the worries of the future and the regrets of the past and into the experience of the moment. Take a moment to experience the difference between how it feels to be thinking about the future or past and how it feels to be thinking only of the present moment. Try this simple experiment. Think about where you want to be and what you want to be doing in 10 years. Tune in to how you feel. Do you feel a bit anxious, or do you feel calm? How does your body feel? Are you a little tense or completely relaxed? Do the same exercise while thinking about your life one year from now, one day from now, in this moment. When you think about what your life will be like in 10 years and then think about what you are doing right now, which feels more relaxed? When you are truly aware of the present moment, there is very little stress. You are going to have thoughts or worries of the future and regrets of the past: it is how your mind functions. However, having most of your thoughts caught up in worry or regret keeps you out of balance, out of awareness of the present moment. The present moment is all that is real; it is the only time in your life when you have control: control to make different choices, control to relax.

Meditation is the practice of bringing your thoughts back home to the present moment. It is the practice of restoring balance: balance of mind and therefore, because of reciprocating influences, balance of body. Through meditation you learn to focus your attention on the body by focusing your attention on your breath. This brings your attention to the present moment because your body lives, and lives only, in the present moment. Bringing your attention to the body, you become more aware of how it is feeling: tense or relaxed. These sensations give you a clue about what your true experience is in the moment. In this awareness you have the opportunity to change your experience. Rather than suppressing or denying feelings and allowing stress to burden your body, you are able to acknowledge how you feel and to choose to release the stress.

Mindful Meditation

Meditation is the optimal stress-management technique. It is the process by which you connect with your deep inner peace. Just as you need to exercise regularly, so too do you need to meditate consistently to experience the conditioning benefits. As you physically train to maintain a certain physical appearance, a certain outlook, so too do you need to condition your thoughts to maintain a certain outlook, a certain posture. Through meditation you learn to be aware of your thoughts and to be quiet in the midst of them. You are not looking to change the thoughts or to push them away. Judging them is resistance, and resistance creates stress. You simply want to observe your thoughts, accept them, and allow them. This practice helps you to become aware of the types of thoughts you have and how you truly feel about life's experiences. Often our negative thoughts and feelings come from issues deep within and not so much from what is happening outside. As you gain a deeper understanding and acceptance of yourself and your perceptions through meditation you gain a greater sense of perspective: what really is important, what you can truly do something about, why you choose to worry, why you choose to be stressed. In meditation you are able to observe your thoughts and become curious about what you fear and why. Being in the presence of your fear, you realize it is merely a thought, one that holds no reality. You gain control by gaining a more relaxed and trusting perspective of yourself, of others, and of life's experiences.

Mindful meditation is the practice of learning the art of *mindful nondoing*. It is the practice of *being*. We are often conditioned to be *doers* and therefore have little balance of *being*. You need both, doing and being, for life to be filled with rapture and true passion. Meditation is the practice of stilling the body so that your physical peace may reciprocate and influence your mental peace. Meditation is the practice of healthy breathing and of becoming more aware of, more present with, yourself in the moment. Focusing on the breath helps relax the body and the mind. As with exercise, the more frequent and longer the periods of relaxation and meditation you give yourself, the more quickly and deeply the body and mind will begin to condition to the relaxation response: you will feel less fatigued, less likely to get excited and stressed, less depressed, more energized, and happier about yourself and your life. Moments of relaxation and meditation are very easy to do anywhere, anytime. A minute of deep breathing will immediately calm you down physically, mentally, and emotionally.

◆ Sit quietly and focus on your breath. The breath is the bridge between your body and your mind.

Meditation is the practice of the breath. The first step in meditation is to learn how to become a *better breather*. We tend to be very shallow breathers, breathing from the chest only. This type of breathing becomes aggravated under stress, which promotes tension and in turn accelerates all bodily functions—the stress response. Take a full, deep breath now, and notice the instinctive response of the body and the mind to relax: breathing, heart rate, blood pressure, hormonal output, thoughts - all slow down. The breath is key to mental and physical relaxation for it is the bridge (the spirit) between the mind and body. If you focus on the breath, you focus on your body. The mind and body are one. Focusing on your breath enhances your awareness of the body in the present moment and is true awareness of yourself.

Breathing Techniques

The breath is the present moment for it is the moment of life. There are three distinct types of breathing for purposes of this discussion. Begin by taking full breaths and becoming aware of how your body feels.

Cleansing Breath Take in a full, deep breath through the nose, filling up your belly first, then letting the air fill your chest all the way up into your shoulders. Exhale with a somewhat quick, gentle force through your mouth: say "aaaaaaaaaahhhhhhh." Sense a cleansing or releasing of as much tension as you are conscious of at this time. These breaths can be short or a bit more drawn out, but it is important that they have a gentle force. Try three to five cleansing breaths.

Belly and Chest Breath Take in a full, deep breath through the nose, and draw the breath all the way down into the belly, filling it up so it begins to round like a barrel. Then allow more air to fill and round the chest. At first this may not feel very comfortable, but that will change with practice. This breath is slower and more drawn out than the cleansing breath. Its purpose is to bring more attention to your belly, releasing greater tension while awakening your creative centers. Try three to five belly and chest breaths.

Quiet Breath Try quiet breaths after you have released tension and are in a more meditative state. This breathing is relaxed, deep, and fluid, with little force. Breathe in through the nose, gently filling up your body, then breathe out through the mouth. This type of breathing allows deep relaxation and meditation. Try three to five quiet breaths.

Meditation Techniques

The following steps will help you in your meditation practice.

1. Select a time and place that is peaceful. When your are first learning meditation, a quiet place is very helpful to your focus. However, keep in mind that life is full of noise and distractions and that you are in the practice of learning how to be quiet (not so stressed) in the midst of them. Meditating in a noisy place is an excellent opportunity to practice how to be quiet when everything around you is busy. Allow yourself to become aware of how you feel both mentally and physically in the midst of the noise. As you become aware of your feelings, such as irritation, anger, frustration, or nervousness about the distractions, you will see that they will change. Allow them to ease. Focus on the quiet that surrounds the noise, and the quiet that is within you despite the noise.

2. Bring all your awareness and concentration to your body and to the moment.

3. It is best to try to release any physical tension in order to find a comfortable position for your meditation. A simple full-body stretch, particularly of the neck and shoulders and upper and lower back, will do well to release some of the "kinks." Your body will tell you what to stretch and move. Practice listening to it by doing a mental scan of your body.

Progressive muscle relaxation is also very effective in releasing physical tension. In this process you simply scan through the muscles of your body. Lying down may be the most effective position for the scan. As you focus on each muscle group, contract the muscle(s) as much as possible for about 30 to 45 seconds. Then let the muscle release. The intense contraction will activate a strong relaxation response from the muscle fibers. Begin at your feet and progress through your body to your head and face.

4. Find a position for meditating that feels very relaxing and comfortable: sit cross-legged on the floor, sit tall in a chair with both feet flat on the floor, or lie on your back with your legs bent and your feet flat on the floor. Place your hands, palms up, either in your lap if you are sitting or at your side if you are lying down. Lying on the floor may induce sleepiness, so you may find sitting more effective. What is most important is that your lower back feels relaxed and supported and that your spine is aligned and balanced—lengthen your spine in all positions by reaching through the crown of your head.

5. Now focus your thoughts on your breathing. Notice the air coming into your body through your nose and out through your mouth. Feel your belly expand, rising as you breathe in and falling as you breathe out. Continuing to breathe fully, scan your body for tension and all sensations. Bring your breath into any tense area and exhale from the area, imagining that you are exhaling the tension out. From time to time thoughts will come that will draw your attention away. Do not try to push these thoughts away. Simply allow these thoughts. Be curious, not judgmental, about the types of thoughts these are. As soon as you become aware that you are thinking, remember to bring your focus back to your breathing and the sensations of your body.

6. You may want to try this visualization to help you focus in. Take your mind's eye to your favorite place. It may be at the ocean, on a mountain, in a forest, by a lake, or somewhere else. Allow yourself to look around and see the things that make you feel good, peaceful, and happy in this place. Imagine yourself sitting down in this place. Now bring your focus to your body, and notice how your body feels as you reflect on these visions.

7. You may want to practice meditation for 30 seconds or 30 minutes or 30 days. There is no "right" length of time nor "right" method. The "right" way is what works best for you. If you begin with 30 seconds and enjoy it, you will do it again and again, and soon for longer periods of time. If you only have a moment, get in a comfortable, aligned position, close your eyes, and take several gentle, deep breaths. Every moment of relaxation is a boost to your health and well-being. The commitment to get in the habit of taking a moment, at least, each day to relax will make a great impact on your health and happiness.

When you first begin a meditation practice, the duration of the sitting is not as important as the frequency of it. Sitting quietly for a few moments each day is more effective than sitting once a week for 30 minutes. You will find that your daily practice will become longer because your body, mind, and spirit will enjoy and want it. Try longer meditations on the weekends or when you have more time. See if the experience is any different.

8. End your meditation by gradually sensing your arms and legs. When you are ready, gently open your eyes. Allow yourself to gradually focus on the things around you—sensing, looking, listening. Before you move, take a moment to sense your body now with your eyes open. Enjoy how you feel.

Meditations Following are a few suggested meditations. It is quite simple to make up your own. You may want to make recordings of these so that you can listen and follow along while you meditate. As you record them, keep your voice calm and your rhythm slow.

Meditation 1: In This Moment

Contemplate the following:

Everything is in the now.

In this moment there is peace, serenity, purity.

In this moment am I. I am reunited with my soul.

In this moment I have all that I need for the life I desire.

In this moment is the truth of experience, that which is the rapture of living.

The possibilities are endless.

Excite in the Unknown.

Delight in each moment, for it is now.

Let the Universe provide—trust.

Breathe.

Meditation 2: Forest in Spring Rain

Visualize the following:

See the rays of dawn come through the leaves.

Smell the essence of the bay leaves.

Feel the cool moistness of the morning dew against your skin.

Step upon the rich, dark earth.

Breathe in the light, cool, fresh air.

Hear the whisper through the trees.

See the lush green of the trees' compassionate canopy.

Hear the gentle morning rain begin to fall.

Feel the cool, gentle sting of the drops upon your face.

See the rain sparkle through the rays of the sun.

Breathe.

Meditation 3: Seeing

Sit and thoughtfully observe the following:

Sit on a bluff by the ocean.

Watch the rolling of the waves.

See them breaking upon the shore.

Contemplate their rhythm, their power, their water.

See and sense the water.

Watch the sun setting on the horizon.

Meditation 4: Meditation Walk

Take a walk. Bring your focus to your breathing.

Bring your attention to your body, to the sensations of your posture.

For a few minutes, practice concentrating on each step you take.

Contemplate the movement of your body as you take each step.

Sense your foot falling on the ground.

Sense your legs, your back, your abdomen, your shoulders.

Feel your head balanced on top of your spine.

Bring your awareness to things around you.

Allow your mind to contemplate and wonder.

Additional Stress-Reduction Techniques

Following are some other ideas for managing the stress of every-day living. Try them, or try to think of others that reflect your own interests.

The Nature Connection Being out in nature is a great way to reduce stress and get a new perspective on life. Break away and go some-where beautiful: view a sunset or the stormy ocean; watch the birds; stare at the stars. The nature around you reflects the nature within you. Nature is peaceful and nurturing: natural, balanced, harmonic, whole. It is a part of you. When you acknowledge that, you acknowl-edge all that is balanced, harmonious, and whole within yourself. Nature will teach you greater awareness about yourself. You need only to observe and be open to the feelings that arise within you.

Walking Works! Take a walk in the evening after dinner rather than plopping down in front of the TV. Enjoy the setting sun. Listen to the evening voices. Walking is an excellent form of active relaxation. This rhythmic, full-body exercise stimulates deep, full breathing and large-range-of-motion movements that are very relaxing. Walking is very kind to the body, conditioning it while inducing very little structural impact.

The Pleasure Principle Pursue pleasure and have fun! How can you possibly be stressed when you are having fun? Laugh a lot. Laughing is a guaranteed stress reducer: it releases various chemicals in the brain that help you feel happier. It is also a terrific abdominal conditioner. And laughing is very contagious.

Go on an Adventure! Whitewater rafting, a major camping trip, a long hike, or a ropes course will be so physically challenging that you will not have time to think about your worries or your regrets. You will be so focused on what you are doing that you will experience the present, living in the now.

At Work Taking five minutes to walk around the office or the block and stretch can reenergize you for hours.

Candlelight Reflection Sit in a dark room lighted only by candles and let your mind wander wherever it wants to go. Remember to breathe deeply, especially if anxious thoughts arise. The soft luminescence of the candles and your deep breathing will help your thoughts become less active.

You Are What You Eat Food has a definite effect on your mood. Coffee can make you irritable, whereas turkey may calm you. Pay more attention to how you feel after you eat something. Be aware so as not to aggravate a mood you may be feeling or induce one that you would rather not feel by choosing to eat something that you know may disturb you.

Keep a Journal Keeping a journal is a journey into your deepest thoughts, feelings, dreams, and desires. These are part of your creative self and help to awaken your inner spirit. Your spiritual self is joyous, relaxed, and balanced.

Photography Taking pictures helps you to slow down and notice the beauty in the people and places of the moment. Often it seems we are too busy and stressed to see what's going on in the moment. Taking a picture is great practice in being calm and present.

Take a Deep Breath A full, deep breath will immediately calm you down every time.

Index

About the Author

Patricia A. Kirk has been a fitness instructor since 1985 and has taught fitness walking since 1989. In addition to teaching rugged walking to clients at Rolling Hills Club, a health/fitness facility where she serves as general manager, Patricia frequently educates corporate employees and fitness professionals on the benefits of her walking program. She also leads weekend fitness retreats, during which she teaches rugged walking and presents workshops on nutrition, fitness and health, and stress reduction.

Patricia holds a Masters degree in exercise science and cardiac rehabilitation from Northeastern Illinois University. She is an ACE Certified Instructor and a former member of the ACE Instructor Certification Exam Committee. She is a board member of U.C. Berkeley's Advisory Committee for Health and Fitness Management Certification Program. She also is a member of both the International Health and Racquet Sports Association and the International Dance Exercise Association.

Patricia currently lives in Novato, California. Her interests include writing, hiking, mountain biking, and photography.